AUDUBON

Wild Bird Desk Diary 1994

JANUARY
S	M	T	W	T	F	S
						1
2	3	4	5	6	7	8
9	10	11	12	13	14	15
16	17	18	19	20	21	22
23	24	25	26	27	28	29
30	31					

FEBRUARY
S	M	T	W	T	F	S
		1	2	3	4	5
6	7	8	9	10	11	12
13	14	15	16	17	18	19
20	21	22	23	24	25	26
27	28					

MARCH
S	M	T	W	T	F	S
		1	2	3	4	5
6	7	8	9	10	11	12
13	14	15	16	17	18	19
20	21	22	23	24	25	26
27	28	29	30	31		

APRIL
S	M	T	W	T	F	S
					1	2
3	4	5	6	7	8	9
10	11	12	13	14	15	16
17	18	19	20	21	22	23
24	25	26	27	28	29	30

MAY
S	M	T	W	T	F	S
1	2	3	4	5	6	7
8	9	10	11	12	13	14
15	16	17	18	19	20	21
22	23	24	25	26	27	28
29	30	31				

JUNE
S	M	T	W	T	F	S
			1	2	3	4
5	6	7	8	9	10	11
12	13	14	15	16	17	18
19	20	21	22	23	24	25
26	27	28	29	30		

JULY
S	M	T	W	T	F	S
					1	2
3	4	5	6	7	8	9
10	11	12	13	14	15	16
17	18	19	20	21	22	23
24	25	26	27	28	29	30
31						

AUGUST
S	M	T	W	T	F	S
	1	2	3	4	5	6
7	8	9	10	11	12	13
14	15	16	17	18	19	20
21	22	23	24	25	26	27
28	29	30	31			

SEPTEMBER
S	M	T	W	T	F	S
				1	2	3
4	5	6	7	8	9	10
11	12	13	14	15	16	17
18	19	20	21	22	23	24
25	26	27	28	29	30	

OCTOBER
S	M	T	W	T	F	S
						1
2	3	4	5	6	7	8
9	10	11	12	13	14	15
16	17	18	19	20	21	22
23	24	25	26	27	28	29
30	31					

NOVEMBER
S	M	T	W	T	F	S
		1	2	3	4	5
6	7	8	9	10	11	12
13	14	15	16	17	18	19
20	21	22	23	24	25	26
27	28	29	30			

DECEMBER
S	M	T	W	T	F	S
				1	2	3
4	5	6	7	8	9	10
11	12	13	14	15	16	17
18	19	20	21	22	23	24
25	26	27	28	29	30	31

Snowy egret (*Egretta thula*) searching for food. Ding Darling National Wildlife Refuge, Sanibel Island, Florida. Nikon F4 with 500mm lens, Fujichrome Velvia at 1/250 second/F5.6. By Barbara Gerlach.

AUDUBON

Wild Bird Desk Diary 1994

MACMILLAN PUBLISHING COMPANY *New York*

MAXWELL MACMILLAN CANADA *Toronto*

MAXWELL MACMILLAN INTERNATIONAL
New York Oxford Singapore Sydney

Northern cardinal (*Cardinalis cardinalis*) surrounded by Spanish moss
(*Tillandsia usneoides*). Armand Bayou near East Galveston Bay, Texas. Nikon F3
with 600mm lens, Kodachrome 64 at 1/60 second/F5.6. By Eleanor Brown.

Photo editing by Monica B. Lamontagne.
Creative supervision by
Wendy G. Batteau.
Text by John Farrand, Jr.
Design by Janet Tingey.
Production by Camillo LoGiudice.
Production editing by Andrew Attaway.
Display lettering by Julian Waters.

Jewish holidays begin at sunset on the
previous evening.
Astronomical information is given in
Eastern Standard Time and Eastern
Daylight Time (when applicable).
Eclipses noted are visible from the
Americas.

Front cover: Male rufous hummingbird (*Selasphorus rufus*) feeding on columbine
(*Aquilegia* sp.). Near Hope, British Columbia, Canada. Nikon F4 with 200mm lens,
Kodachrome 64 at 1/250 second/F22. By Wayne Lankinen.

A Review

From *The Audubon Magazine* February 1887, Issue Number 1

THE AUDUBON SOCIETY was founded by the *Forest and Stream* in February, 1886, with the object of saving the birds of this continent, and especially song and other small birds, from being practically exterminated. Those who thought about the matter saw that the birds were rapidly growing fewer. Many of the farmers noticed that there were not so many birds as there used to be. As a rule they did not trouble themselves much about it; they had too many other things to think of. But sometimes, when their orchards were attacked by insects, and every apple had a worm at its core, or when their crops, one after the other, were damaged by various insects, they recollected that birds eat insects by the thousand, and could not help wondering how it would fare with the harvests if there were no birds left to keep the insects in check.

There were other people besides farmers who lived in the country, or visited it in the summer months, because they liked to get away from the noise, and heat, and dust of the great cities, and spend weeks or months in the woods and fields, and listen to the glad music of the song-birds. These were the first to notice the disappearance of the birds, and to feel the loss deeply. Then there were scientific men, like the members of the American Ornithologists' Union, who make a study of birds and their habits—of the food they eat, and of the share of the world's work which falls upon their shoulders, and who knew that a country could not be deprived of its birds without inflicting very severe trouble upon the people. In fact, it was they, and such as they, who first opened the farmer's eyes to the value of the services which the birds render him, by feeding on insects, and thus saving his whole crop from destruction.

When it was noticed that the birds were not as plenty as they used to be, there was not much difficulty in accounting for it. In the year 1786 there were less than five millions of people in the United States, and the ladies wore no feathers—at least nothing but ostrich or marabout feathers—but in the year 1886 there were fifty-five millions of people in the country—nearly all the ladies wore bird skins or heads or wings; many men went shooting small birds to make money by selling the skins, and innumerable boys went bird nesting. Of course there were exceptions—there were gentle women who were deeply pained at the sight of so many bright lives being thoughtlessly sacrificed; there were men, too, indignant at the wanton destruction of life. But what could one person, or a score of persons do to influence the conduct of a whole people? How could one person appeal to fifty-five millions of people, and ask them even to consider the matter?

Of course the thing was possible, and what is more, it is in a fair way of being achieved. There is hardly a State or Territory in the Union, in which there is not now a large number of people pledged to protect the birds; and there is every reason to believe that before many years shall have passed, a person who has not heard of the movement will be a rare exception.

The idea of founding the Audubon Society originated with Dr. George Bird Grinnell of the Forest and Stream Publishing Company, of New York. As a member of the American Ornithologists' Union, he had acquainted himself with all the facts bearing upon the destruction of birds and their rapid disappearance, and had given much study to the subject in all its aspects. The Union, while it laid stress upon the importance of public agitation for the preservation of our birds, declared plainly that it would not head such a movement. As experts, its members felt warranted in giving time and knowledge freely, and in suggesting measures, but for the circulation of their suggestions to the general public, they appealed to philanthropists, societies and individuals. The papers on this subject read before the A.O.U. were of great interest, and were published as a supplement to *Science*. But it was reserved for Dr. Grinnell to take up the matter from the practical standpoint. Again it was not easy to calculate what it would cost to set on foot a popular movement for the protection of our birds. Most of the warmest friends of the movement held such exaggerated views of what it would cost, that all shrank from committing themselves to any share of the responsibility. To the business managers of the *Forest and Stream* it looked less formidable. They could estimate costs, and if necessary regulate them. They could use their own paper to scatter the seeds of the movement in every State of the Union; it was a movement calculated to secure the co-operation of the press; and seeing one of their own colleagues so anxious to set it afloat, they made the necessary appropriation. On the 13th of February, 1886, the Audubon Society was founded by *Forest and Stream,* and a great number of the leading people of the country were called on to express their sentiments on the subject, or to aid the movement with their hearty co-operation. . . .

The correspondence of the year has been very interesting. Many of the more active lady members who formerly wore feathers, simply because it was the fashion, were quite shocked when they learned from the circulars of the Audubon Society what a fearful sacrifice of bird life was entailed, and how very serious were the future consequences involved; and the last few months have given abundant evidence of the widespread influence of the movement.

It would be hard to say whether boys or girls have behaved most generously in the matter. To both sexes membership in the Audubon Society involves some self-denial for conscience sake, and they have both responded in a manner to maintain the high character of the race and its readiness to place principle above everything.

It was intended to make the Audubon movement a national one, but it has outgrown the conception of its promoters and become a continental one. . . .

The movement appeals so strongly to all intelligent people on economic and humane grounds that it can scarcely fail of accomplishing its objects. These are the education of our whole people to an understanding of the usefulness of the birds and the folly of permitting their wholesale destruction.

Northern mockingbird (*Mimus polyglottos*) perched on winterberry holly
(*Ilex verticillata*). Duanesburg, New York. Nikon 8008 with 600mm lens,
Kodachrome 64 at 1/125 second/F11. By J. Michael Fuller.

How to Become a Birder

E A C H Y E A R thousands of people take up bird-watching, or bird-ing, joining the estimated seven million who are already engaged in this fascinating hobby or sport. They are drawn to it by the appear-ance of a striking or unfamiliar bird in the yard, the gift of a feeder or bird guide, an invitation from a friend to go birding, or the search for an engaging outdoor pastime for the children.

Some people get so involved in birding that they spend every waking hour in the field, planning their next outing or comparing notes with their fellow birders. Others just maintain bird feeders in their gardens or even on city fire escapes, enjoying the sparrows, starlings, doves, and house finches that come for seeds or suet. What-ever time and effort you invest in birding, you will be richly re-warded.

To get started, you need relatively little in the way of equipment, and you already own the most important—sharp eyes, sharp ears, or both. There are many visually impaired birders who find and identify their birds by ear. But the two main pieces of equipment you'll need are a pair of binoculars and a reliable field guide to the birds of your area.

There are binoculars priced to suit every budget, but what counts as much as the binoculars themselves are the skill and dedication of the person using them. In choosing a pair of binoculars that is good for birding, look for such numbers as 7×35, 8×40, or 10×50. The number before the $\times$ is the magnification; a pair of 7×35s will mag-nify the bird seven times, while 10×50s will magnify the image ten times. The number after the $\times$, the 40 in 8×40, is the diameter of the outer lens and governs the amount of light that enters the glasses. The best numbers are about five times the magnification; these let in enough light to enable you to make out colors in deep woods, but not so much that colors are bleached out on a brilliantly sunlit beach. Try out various models to find one that is comfortable for you.

Several excellent field guides are available, some illustrated with paintings of birds and others with photographs. Visit a bookstore and pick out the guide that seems easiest to use. After you've taken it into the field a few times and understand how it works, you will be identifying birds quickly and accurately. If you take up birding seriously, you will eventually own all the guides.

Birding by yourself has its rewards—many of our best birders began as youngsters who didn't know anyone else who was interested in birds—but you'll learn your birds faster if you join experienced birders, who are almost invariably friendly and eager to help beginners. Most towns have bird clubs, which can be located by inquiring at your local public library or natural history museum.

The first thing most birders do is to begin listing the birds they have spotted—compiling a "life list" of all the species they have seen since they started. Some birders keep year's lists, state lists, yard lists (birds they have seen in their own yard), and locality lists. List keeping is fun and it helps you sharpen your skill at identification. It's fascinating to compare your lists from different years or share them with other birders.

Once you've tracked down nearly every bird that occurs in your area and know your birds well—this will happen sooner than you think—you'll probably be inspired to expand your activities. You can become involved in conservation work, take an active role in the organization of your bird club, or participate in Christmas Bird Counts, which are sponsored every year by the National Audubon Society. Some birders even conduct studies of some aspect of the life of birds or of some particular species and publish their findings in scientific journals. There is still much we don't know about even the common species; ornithology is one of the few sciences in which valuable contributions to our knowledge can be made by people with no technical training.

But whatever your degree of involvement in birding, you'll certainly enjoy it. You'll be in tune with some of the earth's interesting creatures. You'll see beautiful and fascinating things that most people never notice.

A great naturalist once said: "We see only what we appreciate, and we appreciate only what we understand." He wasn't talking specifically about birds, but no statement can be applied more aptly to birds and the people who watch them, the birders.

December 1993 / January 1994

D E C E M B E R						
S	M	T	W	T	F	S
			1	2	3	4
5	6	7	8	9	10	11
12	13	14	15	16	17	18
19	20	21	22	23	24	25
26	27	28	29	30	31	

J A N U A R Y						
S	M	T	W	T	F	S
						1
2	3	4	5	6	7	8
9	10	11	12	13	14	15
16	17	18	19	20	21	22
23/30	24/31	25	26	27	28	29

27 MONDAY

28 TUESDAY
Full Moon
◯

29 WEDNESDAY

30 THURSDAY

31 FRIDAY

1 SATURDAY
New Year's Day

2 SUNDAY

Steller's jay (*Cyanocitta stelleri*). Vancouver Island, British Columbia, Canada.
Nikon F4 with 600mm lens, Kodachrome 64 at 1/250 second/F8.
By Wayne Lankinen.

January 1994

			JANUARY			
S	M	T	W	T	F	S
						1
2	3	4	5	6	7	8
9	10	11	12	13	14	15
16	17	18	19	20	21	22
23/30	24/31	25	26	27	28	29

3   MONDAY

4   TUESDAY   Last Quarter ◐

5   WEDNESDAY

6   THURSDAY

7   FRIDAY

8   SATURDAY

9   SUNDAY

January 1994

MONDAY *10*

New Moon
●

TUESDAY *11*

WEDNESDAY *12*

THURSDAY *13*

FRIDAY *14*

SATURDAY *15*

SUNDAY *16*

January 1994

		JANUARY				
S	M	T	W	T	F	S
						1
2	3	4	5	6	7	8
9	10	11	12	13	14	15
16	17	18	19	20	21	22
23/30	24/31	25	26	27	28	29

17 MONDAY   Martin Luther King, Jr.'s
                                                  Birthday *observed*

18 TUESDAY

19 WEDNESDAY   First Quarter
                                                         ◐

20 THURSDAY

21 FRIDAY

22 SATURDAY

23 SUNDAY

Painted bunting (*Passerina ciris*) eating grass seeds. Echo Pond, Everglades National Park, Florida. Nikon F4 with 300mm lens, Fujichrome 100 at 1/250 second/F5.6. By Brian Kenney.

- Many owls have such keen hearing that they can pinpoint the exact location—both the distance and the direction—of a sound made by their prey.

- Grebes are expert divers, but sometimes they avoid danger by sinking slowly out of sight, leaving only their bills protruding above the surface so they can breathe.

- Shrikes are well known for impaling their prey on thorns and barbed wire. It has recently been suggested that they do this not to store food, but to stake claim to territory.

- The zone-tailed hawk of the American Southwest has long, narrow wings and tail like a turkey vulture, and sneaks up on its prey by mimicking this harmless scavenger.

- The osprey, a fish-eating hawk, has sharp spines on the undersides of its toes for grasping its slippery prey.

- City pigeons, domestic descendants of the wild rock dove, come in a variety of colors, but not because of selective breeding by humans. They can develop such variations, which would be risky in the wild, because they have few predators in cities.

- The female brown-headed cowbird lays her eggs in the nests of other birds, usually one per nest; in any one season, she lays up to twelve eggs. The yellow warbler has a clever defense against unwanted cowbird eggs. It simply lays down a new lining covering up the alien egg and starts a new set of eggs of its own. One enterprising female warbler was found to have done this six times in a single nest.

- Unlike the European cuckoo, the yellow-billed cuckoo of North America only rarely lays its eggs in the nests of other birds. This nest parasitism is most likely to occur during heavy infestations of tent caterpillars, when an abundance of food triggers an overproduction of eggs; the extra eggs are laid in nests of the black-billed cuckoo. Not to be outdone, the black-billed cuckoo places its extra eggs in nests of the yellow-billed cuckoo.

January 1994

J A N U A R Y						
S	M	T	W	T	F	S
						1
2	3	4	5	6	7	8
9	10	11	12	13	14	15
16	17	18	19	20	21	22
23/30	24/31	25	26	27	28	29

MONDAY 24

TUESDAY 25

WEDNESDAY 26

Full Moon
○

THURSDAY 27

FRIDAY 28

SATURDAY 29

SUNDAY 30

Winter Visitors

EVERY WINTER, when most of our breeding birds have gone south in search of a reliable food supply, we are visited by a host of species from farther north, by birds that can still find sufficient food despite the harsh weather. This is the time to keep the bird feeder stocked and put on extra layers of clothing so you can go out and see birds you won't find during any other season. Even in the warmest regions of the United States, the change of seasons will bring a change in the range of species you can see.

Many of these winter visitors put in an appearance every year. Brown creepers, kinglets, longspurs, white-throated sparrows, tree sparrows, and juncos can be counted on to show up in areas south of their nesting grounds when cold weather arrives. There are many other birds for which a normal winter in the Arctic or in Canada poses no threat, who can find abundant food even when the thermometer reads well below zero. But when their food supply gives out, these birds stage what ornithologists call an irruption, invading the northern United States in large numbers.

Such irruptive birds fall into two categories. Some predatory birds —hawks and owls—are dependent on just a few kinds of prey during the winter, and if their prey suffers a population crash, then the predator has little choice but to fly south in search of new hunting grounds. Since prey populations tend to crash on a regular schedule, these predatory birds show up at more or less regular intervals. For example, the snowy owl, the most celebrated predatory bird of the Far North, feeds almost exclusively on lemmings and voles, whose populations tend to plummet about once every four years. If the population crash is a mild one, only the young birds—heavily flecked with black—fly south, but during a major crash even the adults, including the all-white adult males, may show up. The last major irruption of snowy owls took place in the winter of 1991–92, so if things proceed according to schedule, we can expect another invasion in the winter of 1995–96.

Other predators that must fly south from time to time are the rough-legged hawk and the northern shrike, which are also dependent on lemmings and voles, and the northern goshawk, a big, blue-gray predator that relies on the snowshoe hare. Snowshoe hares suffer population crashes roughly every ten years, so goshawks turn up in larger than normal numbers about once a decade.

Nonpredatory birds tend to show up less frequently. Red-breasted nuthatches and several species of northern finches, for example, survive the winter by feeding on berries or the seeds of conifers in Canada's vast forests—crops that fail at irregular intervals. And crop failures may only be local; the birds may be able to find another feeding area without leaving the Canadian forests. Then, too, there is never a universal failure of all food sources, so there is never a year when Bohemian and cedar waxwings, pine and evening grosbeaks, black-capped and boreal chickadees, redbreasted nuthatches, pine siskins, common and hoary redpolls, purple finches, and red and white-winged crossbills all appear at once. So we don't know that there is going to be an irruption of seed-eaters or berry-eaters until the birds arrive.

In a given year, there may be lots of red-breasted nuthatches, indicating a widespread failure of conifer seeds, but not a sign of redpolls, meaning that birches and alders produced a good seed crop. Our regular birding area may suddenly be invaded by red crossbills, a fact that tells us that somewhere to the north, the pines produced no seeds, or by white-winged crossbills, which means that it is the crop of seeds of spruces and firs that has failed.

For birders, half the fun of waiting for winter is wondering what irruptive species will show up to delight them.

January /
February 1994

		J	A	N	U	A	R	Y	
S	M	T	W	T	F	S
						1
2	3	4	5	6	7	8
9	10	11	12	13	14	15
16	17	18	19	20	21	22
23/30	24/31	25	26	27	28	29

		F	E	B	R	U	A	R	Y	
S	M	T	W	T	F	S
		1	2	3	4	5
6	7	8	9	10	11	12
13	14	15	16	17	18	19
20	21	22	23	24	25	26
27	28					

31 MONDAY

1 TUESDAY

2 WEDNESDAY

3 THURSDAY

Last Quarter

4 FRIDAY

5 SATURDAY

6 SUNDAY

Snowy owl (*Nyctea scandiaca*) in flight. Near Metcalf National Wildlife Refuge, Montana. Canon EOS 1, Kodachrome 64 at 1/250 second/F4. By Alan and Sandy Carey.

February 1994

FEBRUARY						
S	M	T	W	T	F	S
		1	2	3	4	5
6	7	8	9	10	11	12
13	14	15	16	17	18	19
20	21	22	23	24	25	26
27	28					

7 MONDAY

8 TUESDAY

9 WEDNESDAY

10 THURSDAY   New Moon
                              ●

11 FRIDAY

12 SATURDAY

13 SUNDAY

Valentine's Day

MONDAY *14*

TUESDAY *15*

Ash Wednesday

WEDNESDAY *16*

THURSDAY *17*

First Quarter
◐

FRIDAY *18*

SATURDAY *19*

SUNDAY *20*

February 1994

FEBRUARY						
S	M	T	W	T	F	S
		1	2	3	4	5
6	7	8	9	10	11	12
13	14	15	16	17	18	19
20	21	22	23	24	25	26
27	28					

21 MONDAY   Presidents' Day

22 TUESDAY

23 WEDNESDAY

24 THURSDAY

25 FRIDAY   Full Moon

26 SATURDAY

27 SUNDAY

Young male pine grosbeak (*Pinicola enucleator*) perched on white spruce
(*Picea glauca*). Near Thunder Bay, Ontario, Canada. Nikon F4 with 600mm lens,
Kodachrome 64 at 1/250 second/F8. By Wayne Lankinen.

- The world champion long-distance migrant was an Arctic tern that was banded as a nestling at Disko Bay on the west coast of Greenland on July 8, 1951, and found dead on the east coast of South Africa, 11,000 miles away, 105 days later.

- The record for sustained speed is held by a semipalmated sandpiper that was banded in Massachusetts in August 1985 and was shot by a hunter in Guyana—2,750 miles away—four days later. To have traveled this far so fast, the bird must have maintained an average flight speed of more than 28 miles per hour.

- The fastest animal in the world is the peregrine falcon; during a dive in pursuit of prey it may attain a speed of 217 miles per hour.

- The largest bird's nest on record belonged to a pair of bald eagles near St. Petersburg, Florida. It weighed more than 6,700 pounds, and was 20 feet deep and nearly 10 feet wide.

- The longest-lived wild North American bird on record was an Arctic tern that survived for 34 years.

- After the domestic chicken, the world's most abundant bird is probably the Wilson's storm-petrel, a frail seabird that breeds by the millions in the subantarctic and spends the southern winter at sea in the oceans of the northern hemisphere.

- The smallest owl in North America is the well-named elf owl; this denizen of the southwestern deserts is no bigger than a house sparrow. The largest North American owl is the great gray, a rare species of the Far North that seldom visits the United States.

- The lightest North American bird is the Calliope hummingbird, which weighs in at one-tenth of an ounce. The heaviest is the trumpeter swan, which averages thirty pounds, or about 4,800 times the weight of a Calliope hummingbird.

FEBRUARY

S	M	T	W	T	F	S
		1	2	3	4	5
6	7	8	9	10	11	12
13	14	15	16	17	18	19
20	21	22	23	24	25	26
27	28					

MARCH

S	M	T	W	T	F	S
		1	2	3	4	5
6	7	8	9	10	11	12
13	14	15	16	17	18	19
20	21	22	23	24	25	26
27	28	29	30	31		

February / March 1994

MONDAY *28*

TUESDAY *1*

WEDNESDAY *2*

THURSDAY *3*

Last Quarter
◐

FRIDAY *4*

SATURDAY *5*

SUNDAY *6*

Summer Residents Start to Arrive

BY THE END of February, the average birder has had enough of winter and is waiting patiently—or impatiently—for the return of warm weather and the birds that return with it. That patience is finally rewarded in March.

To be sure, a few signs of spring appear earlier. In much of the country, great horned owls begin nesting—and hooting loudly on moonlit nights—as early as January. In the Northeast, house finches usually begin singing in the middle of February, and mourning doves start to coo at about the same time. In coastal California, the rufous-sided towhees may begin singing as early as January, and Anna's hummingbirds, scrub jays, and house finches may even begin nesting in February. Along the coast of Texas, the purple martins usually arrive before February has ended and begin their throaty warbling in the pre-dawn darkness. And some of the winter birds quietly begin to disappear, among them snow buntings, horned larks, and tree sparrows. But a birder's cabin fever is best relieved by the sight of a bird he knows has newly returned from farther south.

The list of such early arrivals is not long, especially now that winters are warmer and more species can be seen in every month of the year. In the Northeast, such harbingers of spring include northern flickers, red-winged blackbirds, common grackles, American robins, and eastern phoebes. Around San Francisco, Allen's hummingbirds, violet-green swallows, house wrens, and orange-crowned warblers are on the list of March arrivals. Farther south, on the Gulf Coast, the list is longer, and includes birds that won't make it to the northern states for a month or more; here one can find wood thrushes, red-eyed vireos, black-and-white warblers, Baltimore orioles, and indigo buntings.

These March migrants move north slowly, making advances as the weather permits. A prolonged cold spell can stall their northward movement for long periods. In any one place the dates of their arrival may vary by several weeks in different years. Migrants arriving later in the season, in mid-May for example, may appear on or near the same date in any given year.

But even with this careful progress northward there are risks. Insects, abundant when these birds arrived, may fall prey to an unexpected sharp frost. Redwings, grackles, thrushes, and orioles can switch to a diet of seeds or fruit—if they can find them in time—but for phoebes, vireos, or warblers caught without a supply of insects and faced with low temperatures, the result may be starvation.

A sudden winter storm can spell disaster. On the night of March 13, 1904, a heavy, wet snowstorm moving southward across the Great Plains collided with a large, northbound migration of Lapland longspurs in the Midwest, resulting in an estimated five million casualties. The next morning, the bodies of 750,000 longspurs were found scattered over the ice of just two small lakes in Minnesota. More localized tragedies also occur. A spring ice storm can wipe out all the newly arrived male eastern phoebes in an area.

Fortunately, these first arrivals are common species that can build up their numbers in a short time. For phoebes, a later group of males can arrive and take over the nesting territories left by the birds that have died. Even the effects of the great longspur disaster of 1904 were short-lived; within a few years after those five million had been killed, numbers were back to normal.

So birders can go into the field and enjoy their first spring sightings without too much worry. That red-winged blackbird singing in its accustomed cattail marsh, the party of common grackles flying rapidly through a neighborhood, a wood thrush in a swampy thicket south of New Orleans, or the first robin darting across the lawn may well mean that winter is about to release its grip, or already has.

March 1994

MARCH						
S	M	T	W	T	F	S
		1	2	3	4	5
6	7	8	9	10	11	12
13	14	15	16	17	18	19
20	21	22	23	24	25	26
27	28	29	30	31		

7 MONDAY

8 TUESDAY

9 WEDNESDAY

10 THURSDAY

11 FRIDAY

12 SATURDAY   New Moon

                                                        ●

13 SUNDAY

Black-crowned night heron (*Nycticorax nycticorax*). Delaware Bay near Little Creek, Delaware. Nikon 8008 with 600mm lens, Fujichrome 100 at 1/250 second/F5.6. By C. Gable Ray.

March 1994

			MARCH			
S	M	T	W	T	F	S
		1	2	3	4	5
6	7	8	9	10	11	12
13	14	15	16	17	18	19
20	21	22	23	24	25	26
27	28	29	30	31		

14 MONDAY

15 TUESDAY

16 WEDNESDAY

17 THURSDAY   St. Patrick's Day

18 FRIDAY

19 SATURDAY

20 SUNDAY   First Quarter

◐

Equinox

MONDAY *21*

TUESDAY *22*

WEDNESDAY *23*

THURSDAY *24*

FRIDAY *25*

SATURDAY *26*

SUNDAY *27*

Full Moon

◯

Palm Sunday
Passover

March /
April 1994

MARCH						
S	M	T	W	T	F	S
		1	2	3	4	5
6	7	8	9	10	11	12
13	14	15	16	17	18	19
20	21	22	23	24	25	26
27	28	29	30	31		

APRIL						
S	M	T	W	T	F	S
					1	2
3	4	5	6	7	8	9
10	11	12	13	14	15	16
17	18	19	20	21	22	23
24	25	26	27	28	29	30

28 MONDAY

29 TUESDAY

30 WEDNESDAY

31 THURSDAY

1 FRIDAY

Good Friday

2 SATURDAY

Last Quarter

3 SUNDAY

Easter
Daylight Saving
Time Begins

Tundra swans (*Cygnus columbianus*) in flight. Blackwater National Wildlife Refuge, Maryland. Nikon 8008 with 300mm lens, Fujichrome 50 at 1/250 second/F5.6. By C. Gable Ray.

Spring Migration

MOST NORTH AMERICAN birds are migratory. It has been estimated that of the 215 species that nest in Michigan, only twenty, or 9 percent, do not migrate. Following the trickle of birds that arrives in March, the spring migration soon swells to a flood. Whether they have wintered in the southern United States as eastern bluebirds do; in Argentina, as bobolinks do; or in the Antarctic, as Arctic terns do, birds hurry northward to nest.

Responding to changes in day length, wintering birds put on a layer of fat to serve as fuel and acquire their breeding plumage for the journey. Some birds, mainly small birds that fly well, such as hummingbirds, swallows, and swifts, as well as larger vultures, hawks, eagles, storks, pelicans, and cranes, migrate during the day. Others, among them water birds like ducks, geese, swans, shorebirds, and loons, travel both day and night. It is these diurnal and day-and-night travelers that we can actually see in the act of migrating.

But the majority of migrants are small songbirds, and most of these travel only under the cover of darkness, when they are safe from such predators as falcons. Despite their small size, many of these songbirds travel long distances to reach their breeding grounds in North America; some thrushes and vireos winter in the forests of southern Brazil, south of the Equator, and make northward journeys of as much as 8,000 miles. At the other extreme are birds like juncos and rosy finches that nest high in the mountains of the West; many of these merely descend to the lowlands for the winter, so their journey home may cover less than 100 miles. The mountain quail migrates on foot, trotting single-file up the slopes as warm weather arrives, in what must be one of the shortest migrations of any North American bird. Since it is cooler at higher elevations, a walk of one mile up the mountain is equivalent to a journey of 2,500 miles northward.

A few species, mainly insect-eating shorebirds like the white-rumped sandpiper, lesser yellowlegs, and lesser golden plover, follow different routes in spring and fall. In the spring these birds fly northward from the pampas of Argentina and reach their Arctic nesting grounds by heading up the Great Plains. In the fall, on their return journey, they will fly east to Newfoundland and Nova Scotia, where they fatten up before making a nonstop flight to northern

South America, the first leg of their trip back to Argentina.

The routes of many migrants, especially shorebirds, are nicely timed to place the birds at prime feeding sites just when food is most abundant. Their northward journey consists of stages. The most famous of these is the red knot, which arrives at Delaware Bay in late May, just as the horseshoe crabs are laying their billions of eggs. The red knots arrive with their stores of fat depleted and leave well fueled for the final leg of their journey to the Arctic. If anything were to disrupt this ancient and delicate balance—an oil spill in Delaware Bay, for example—the red knot might never recover.

Again, most of our migrants are small songbirds, and these are insect-eaters. The timing of their travels is governed by the emergence of small insects. The first flush of foliage brings out the insects, and the migrant songbirds are on hand to eat them. The males arrive first, because they must reach the breeding grounds in time to compete for a good nesting territory. The females follow a few days or weeks later.

Radar studies have shown that night-flying songbirds migrate on a broad front, and fly alone rather than in flocks. But we tend to see them in groups because in their northward journey they are channeled and funneled by mountain ranges, rivers, and bays. They also collect where their insect food is most abundant. An experienced birder knows this, and so when he is out searching for migrants he doesn't wander through the woods, but heads for a quiet stream and looks for places where the early morning sun has warmed the foliage of the trees. Here he will find migrants in the greatest number and variety.

April 1994

APRIL

S	M	T	W	T	F	S
					1	2
3	4	5	6	7	8	9
10	11	12	13	14	15	16
17	18	19	20	21	22	23
24	25	26	27	28	29	30

4 MONDAY   Easter Monday (Canada)

5 TUESDAY

6 WEDNESDAY

7 THURSDAY

8 FRIDAY

9 SATURDAY

10 SUNDAY   New Moon
                                                    ●

White-crowned sparrow (*Zonotrichia leucophrys*) feeding on bluet damselfly
(*Enallagma carunculatum*). Langley Township, British Columbia, Canada. Olympus
OM-4T with 350mm lens, Fujichrome Velvia at 1/125 second/F5.6.
By Edwin G. A. Willcox.

April 1994

APRIL						
S	M	T	W	T	F	S
					1	2
3	4	5	6	7	8	9
10	11	12	13	14	15	16
17	18	19	20	21	22	23
24	25	26	27	28	29	30

11 MONDAY

12 TUESDAY

13 WEDNESDAY

14 THURSDAY

15 FRIDAY

16 SATURDAY

17 SUNDAY

First Quarter
◐

MONDAY *18*

TUESDAY *19*

WEDNESDAY *20*

THURSDAY *21*

Earth Day

FRIDAY *22*

SATURDAY *23*

SUNDAY *24*

April /
May 1994

		A P R I L				
S	M	T	W	T	F	S
					1	2
3	4	5	6	7	8	9
10	11	12	13	14	15	16
17	18	19	20	21	22	23
24	25	26	27	28	29	30

		M A Y				
S	M	T	W	T	F	S
1	2	3	4	5	6	7
8	9	10	11	12	13	14
15	16	17	18	19	20	21
22	23	24	25	26	27	28
29	30	31				

25 MONDAY   Full Moon
                                                  ○

26 TUESDAY   John James Audubon's
                                              Birthday

27 WEDNESDAY

28 THURSDAY

29 FRIDAY   Arbor Day

30 SATURDAY

1 SUNDAY

Common yellowthroat (*Geothlypis trichas*). Deal Island Wildlife Management Area, Maryland. Nikon FM2 with 600mm lens, Fujichrome 100 at 1/250 second/F8. By C. Gable Ray.

Warblers

IF YOU ASK a dedicated birder—birders prefer the word "serious"—what his or her favorite time of year is, the answer will probably be the spring migration. But if you press for more details, the answer is likely to be the warbler migration, at least in the eastern half of the country. Warblers, smaller than sparrows and with finely pointed bills, are among the most colorful of North American birds, and while you can't expect to find every one of them in any given spot, fully thirty-eight species migrate through all or part of eastern North America. The migrants tend to come in "waves," pushed forward by southerly winds and held back by winds out of the north. In a big warbler wave in May, if the weather is right and the trees have not yet fully leafed out, it is possible to see as many as two dozen species in a single day.

Some warbler species are confusingly similar in the fall, but in spring each male wears his colors in a distinct pattern. Yellow, green, and black are the most common colors, but some species show orange, chestnut, blue, or gray, and two species are black and white. In the Southwest, the red-faced warbler is bright red on the face and throat, and the painted redstart is attractively patterned in black, white, and red.

No warblers actually warble, but their songs, which consist of trills and high-pitched musical notes, are easy to learn. Some birders, out early on a May morning, can run up a big list of species by relying entirely on their ears.

During the migration most warblers forage high in the trees catching tiny insects that feed on newly emerged, tender leaves; but others, among them the common yellowthroat, skulk in thickets just as they do on the nesting grounds, and a few, including the ovenbird and the two water thrushes, walk about on the ground. One species, the black-and-white warbler, creeps on the trunks of trees like a nuthatch. The best place to look for migrating warblers is in woodlands along streams or, perhaps ironically, in parks in large cities, where the birds are attracted by an island of green in a sea of concrete and steel.

Many warblers continue north on their spring migration and breed in the conifer forests of Canada, but no state is without its nesting warblers. Most build a simple cup of twigs, plant stems, or grass, but the golden-yellow prothonotary warbler nests in holes in trees; the northern parula weaves its nest into a hanging tuft of Spanish moss; and the ovenbird builds a domed, oven-shaped nest on the ground. Most lay four or five spotted eggs, which they incubate for about twelve days, and the young fledge after about two weeks. A few species are known to raise a second brood.

As soon as nesting season is over, the adults molt into their fall plumage. In some species they look the same as they do in spring, but in others they assume a drab, olive-green coat of feathers like that of the young. It is these species that cause confusion during the fall migration.

Since most warblers are birds of woodlands, and since much of eastern North America is wooded, one might think that these birds are in no danger. But warblers face at least three serious threats to their existence. Many species spend the winter in tropical rain forests, which are being cleared at an alarming rate. Warblers are as dependent on their wintering grounds as they are on their nesting grounds. Here at home, woodlands are increasingly being subdivided by shopping malls, housing projects, and airports. It has been found that birds nesting in such fragmented woodlands are much more vulnerable to predators than those that nest in vast, unbroken tracts of forest. Some warblers that try to nest in small woodlots lose all their young every year.

Perhaps the most serious threat to warblers is the brown-headed cowbird, a species that lays its eggs in the nests of other birds and leaves its young to be raised by foster parents. While many warbler species have long been exposed to cowbirds and have evolved defenses against this parasitism, cowbirds have begun to spread into areas where the local birds have no previous experience with them. Here, warblers and other birds often fail to raise any young of their own. At least two species, the golden-cheeked warbler of Texas and Kirtland's warbler of Michigan, are now on the endangered list, largely because of the depredations of cowbirds. Unless we can find a way to protect the warblers from cowbirds, other species may join the list and our colorful migrants may continue to decline.

May 1994

		M	A	Y		
S	M	T	W	T	F	S
1	2	3	4	5	6	7
8	9	10	11	12	13	14
15	16	17	18	19	20	21
22	23	24	25	26	27	28
29	30	31				

2   MONDAY   Last Quarter ◑

3   TUESDAY

4   WEDNESDAY

5   THURSDAY

6   FRIDAY

7   SATURDAY

8   SUNDAY   Mother's Day

Magnolia warbler (*Dendroica magnolia*) mating pair with chicks nesting in balsam fir (*Abies balsamea*). Near Thunder Bay, Ontario, Canada. Nikon F3 with 600mm lens, Kodachrome 64 at 1/60 second/F22. By Robert Lankinen.

May 1994

M A Y						
S	M	T	W	T	F	S
1	2	3	4	5	6	7
8	9	10	11	12	13	14
15	16	17	18	19	20	21
22	23	24	25	26	27	28
29	30	31				

9 MONDAY

10 TUESDAY

New Moon

●

Annular Eclipse of the Sun
10:57 A.M. E.D.T.

11 WEDNESDAY

12 THURSDAY

13 FRIDAY

14 SATURDAY

15 SUNDAY

MONDAY *16*

TUESDAY *17*

First Quarter
◐

WEDNESDAY *18*

THURSDAY *19*

FRIDAY *20*

SATURDAY *21*

SUNDAY *22*

May 1994

			MAY			
S	M	T	W	T	F	S
1	2	3	4	5	6	7
8	9	10	11	12	13	14
15	16	17	18	19	20	21
22	23	24	25	26	27	28
29	30	31				

23 MONDAY   Victoria Day (Canada)

24 TUESDAY   Full Moon
                                                           ○

25 WEDNESDAY

26 THURSDAY

27 FRIDAY

28 SATURDAY

29 SUNDAY

Wilson's plover (*Charadrius wilsonia*) incubating eggs amid railroad vine
(*Ipomoea pes-caprae*). Manasota Key, Florida. Nikon F4 with 400mm lens, Fujichrome
100 at 1/500 second/F3.5. By Brian Kenney.

- The red-cockaded woodpecker nests in holes in trees, but provides added protection for its eggs and young by drilling sap holes around its nest entrance. The oozing sap keeps predators, even tree-climbing snakes, from reaching the entrance of the nest.

- If it is alarmed, a chickadee incubating its eggs at the bottom of a tree cavity utters a loud hiss that sounds enough like a snake to scare off many a would-be predator.

- Kittiwakes are the only gulls that nest on sea cliffs; unlike the young of other gulls, nestling kittiwakes do not try to flee when they are disturbed but crouch in the nest, thereby avoiding a fatal tumble from the narrow ledge.

- The ovenbird is named for the shape of its nest, a small structure of leaves and twigs with an entrance in the side, shaped like an old-fashioned Dutch oven.

- American robins line their nests with a sturdy wall of dried mud. A nesting female robin can often be identified by the mud she wears on her breast, acquired when she sat in the nest and slowly turned, giving the nest its shape.

- Female bobwhites sometimes lay their eggs together in the same nest; one nest was found that contained 40 eggs.

- Tufted titmice raise more than one brood a season, and the young of earlier broods sometimes help their parents to feed and care for the young of later broods.

- Young eiders gather into groups called crèches, which contain members of several broods and are tended by several females.

- Most birds have one or two brood patches, areas of bare skin that are used to warm the eggs during incubation. Pelicans and gannets, which have no brood patches, wrap the eggs in their feet, and warm them using blood vessels in the webs.

M A Y						
S	M	T	W	T	F	S
1	2	3	4	5	6	7
8	9	10	11	12	13	14
15	16	17	18	19	20	21
22	23	24	25	26	27	28
29	30	31				

J U N E						
S	M	T	W	T	F	S
			1	2	3	4
5	6	7	8	9	10	11
12	13	14	15	16	17	18
19	20	21	22	23	24	25
26	27	28	29	30		

Memorial Day

MONDAY 30

TUESDAY 31

Last Quarter

WEDNESDAY 1

THURSDAY 2

FRIDAY 3

SATURDAY 4

SUNDAY 5

Nesting

WHEN THE spring migration is finally over, and the local birds have settled down to raise their young, most birders hang up their binoculars and wait for the fall migration to start. They know that rare birds will be even rarer now, and that their daily lists will be shorter. But while there are fewer birds around without the migrants, those that are around are dependable. You can watch them day after day and learn their songs, the details of their plumages, and their distinctive habits and behavior. The nesting season is the time to really get to know the birds.

There is more to nesting than building a nest, laying eggs, and raising young. A pair of breeding birds needs an adequate food supply for their young and for themselves, and they also need security. Except for species that nest in colonies, such as gulls, terns, and swallows, which seek their food at some distance from the nest, birds guarantee a food supply by setting up a large territory around the nest and defending it from other members of their own species—potential competitors. Even many colonial birds defend a small territory immediately around the nest, but this is usually to protect nesting material from being stolen or to avoid interference from their inquisitive neighbors. For birds that are not colonial, territories range in size from the many square miles claimed by eagles to a few hundred square yards for small songbirds. It has been found that the richer the supply of food is, the smaller the territory. Song sparrows nesting in poor habitat in the Midwest must defend a territory of thousands of square yards, while members of the same species nesting in the productive salt marshes around San Francisco Bay expend much less energy, defending a territory only a fraction of the size.

Having a territory makes food easier to find in another way. By occupying a relatively small piece of real estate, the nesting pair has a chance to get to know it well and learn where the best feeding places are. They expend less energy in finding food, and so can raise more young.

The chief means of defending a nesting territory are the song and brighter colors of the male. By singing a song that is unique to his species, the male warns away other males. Males quickly learn the individual songs of their neighbors and rarely intrude on one another's territories, so physical combat is rare. During a face-to-face encounter between two rival males, the bright colors are displayed, and the owner of the territory usually succeeds in intimidating the intruder before blows are exchanged.

For security, many species such as terns and auks nest on offshore islands where there are no mammal predators. A few birds, among them the grebes, make islands of their own—nests built of floating vegetation. Others, like some swallows, swifts, and hawks, place their nests on inaccessible cliffs. Eagles and ospreys often nest in the tops of tall trees, where few mammal predators can reach them. Woodpeckers lay their eggs in holes in trees, and many other species use these holes when the woodpeckers have abandoned them. Kingfishers and bank swallows dig burrows in banks beside streams.

Other birds rely on concealment for security. They may build their nests in the dense foliage of a thicket or tree, as do mockingbirds, cardinals, and most warblers, or in a tuft of grass, as most sparrows do. A wood pewee or hummingbird saddles its nest to a limb, where it is often overlooked as part of the branch. A few species place their nests in full view but carefully camouflaged, like plovers on a beach or whippoorwills on the leafy forest floor. In nearly all species the female, who does most of the incubating, is clad in quiet colors to make her hard to spot as she visits the nest or incubates the eggs.

These are the basic needs of a pair of nesting birds, but each species goes about breeding in its own way. In some species, males may defend a large territory that is occupied by more than one female. In the acorn woodpecker, a single female may have several mates. In phalaropes, the spotted sandpiper, and a few other species, the roles of the sexes are reversed; the female defends the territory and the male incubates the eggs and cares for the young. In many species, usually those in which the sexes are colored alike, both parents share equally in all the tasks of nesting, while in some, such as hummingbirds and ducks, the male leaves the female to do it all once mating has occurred.

Variations in breeding styles are as numerous as the birds themselves. To find out what they are, a birder needs only to keep his binoculars handy after the last migrant has disappeared to the north.

June 1994

			JUNE			
S	M	T	W	T	F	S
			1	2	3	4
5	6	7	8	9	10	11
12	13	14	15	16	17	18
19	20	21	22	23	24	25
26	27	28	29	30		

6 MONDAY

7 TUESDAY

8 WEDNESDAY

9 THURSDAY

New Moon

●

10 FRIDAY

11 SATURDAY

12 SUNDAY

Male broad-billed hummingbird (*Cyanthus latirostris*). Saguaro National Monument near Tucson, Arizona. Pentax LX with 400mm lens, Fujichrome 50 at 1/500 second/F2.8. By Adam Jones.

June 1994

			JUNE			
S	M	T	W	T	F	S
			1	2	3	4
5	6	7	8	9	10	11
12	13	14	15	16	17	18
19	20	21	22	23	24	25
26	27	28	29	30		

13 MONDAY

14 TUESDAY

15 WEDNESDAY

16 THURSDAY   First Quarter

17 FRIDAY

18 SATURDAY

19 SUNDAY   Father's Day

MONDAY 20

Solstice

TUESDAY 21

WEDNESDAY 22

Full Moon
○

THURSDAY 23

FRIDAY 24

SATURDAY 25

SUNDAY 26

- The American dipper forages by walking on the bottom of rushing streams, searching for aquatic insects; its plumage is more waterproof than that of any other songbird.

- The snail kite is one of the most specialized of North American birds. It feeds almost exclusively on apple snails (*Pomacea*) and cannot survive in places where these snails are not found.

- Unlike most owls, the northern hawk owl hunts during the day, a useful habit in the Far North, where it doesn't get dark during the summer months.

- Cedar waxwings, birds that feed on berries, sometimes eat fermented fruit growing along the sides of roads; they become intoxicated and are liable to be hit by passing cars.

- Unlike most terns, the gull-billed tern rarely dives for fish, but preys on insects it captures in flight.

- Although it is a woodpecker, the northern flicker spends much of its time on the ground in pursuit of its favorite food—ants.

- Green-winged teal are ducks that sometimes forage far from water. Small flocks have been found walking on the ground in upland woods, searching for acorns.

- Unlike most owls, which swallow their prey whole and then cough up pellets of undigested bones and hair, northern pygmy owls pick the meat from their prey, and so do not have to produce pellets.

- When a family group of scaled quail is busy foraging, the male stands nearby on a rock or mound of earth, on the alert for danger.

- Waterthrushes do most of their foraging in wet places by flipping over leaves or pulling them out of the water, searching for aquatic insects hiding underneath.

J U N E						
S	M	T	W	T	F	S
			1	2	3	4
5	6	7	8	9	10	11
12	13	14	15	16	17	18
19	20	21	22	23	24	25
26	27	28	29	30		

J U L Y						
S	M	T	W	T	F	S
					1	2
3	4	5	6	7	8	9
10	11	12	13	14	15	16
17	18	19	20	21	22	23
24/31	25	26	27	28	29	30

June / July 1994

MONDAY 27

TUESDAY 28

WEDNESDAY 29

Last Quarter

◑

THURSDAY 30

Canada Day

FRIDAY 1

SATURDAY 2

SUNDAY 3

Hummingbirds

HUMMINGBIRDS are unique to the Americas. In all, there are about 320 species, ranging from Alaska to Tierra del Fuego, but only sixteen nest north of the Mexican border, and just a few more put in an occasional appearance. Only one species is common east of the Mississippi; the rest are found in the West and Southwest.

The smallest of all birds, hummingbirds astounded the first European visitors to America. The earliest writers were prone to exaggerate the exoticism of the wildlife in the New World, but there was no need to embellish the facts about these tiny feathered creatures. Some of them are no larger than insects. They glitter like jewels. Their wings beat so fast as to be invisible. And they can hover and fly backwards.

Hummingbirds turn out to be even more remarkable than the first Europeans realized. Feeding almost exclusively on a diet of nectar from flowers and the small insects it contains, they have a higher rate of metabolism than any other living creature, and so must forage almost incessantly to maintain the supply of fuel they require. If you see a hummingbird simply resting, it has probably taken in all the nectar its body can handle, and is waiting to digest some so it can resume visiting flowers.

So dependent are hummingbirds on a steady supply of carbohydrates that they will quickly starve to death if they cannot feed. At night, especially if the temperature drops sharply, they may enter a torpid state in which their heartbeat and rate of respiration slows, in order to conserve energy until daylight comes and they can start feeding again.

Hummingbirds are feisty little birds that vigorously defend beds of nectar-rich flowers. A male hummingbird in possession of a stand of flowers often begins the day by draining the nectar from the flowers around the edge of its territory, so it can spend the rest of the day concentrating its attention on the flowers in the center. And hummingbirds know friend from foe; they drive away not only other hummingbirds, but also bees and hawk moths, which are competing nectar-feeders.

Certain plants specifically aim to woo hummingbirds, because hummingbirds are excellent pollinators—efficient, fast-moving, and wide-ranging. They will take nectar from almost any flower but are especially attracted by the color red; many plants that rely on hummingbirds to spread their pollen, such as cardinal lobelia and trumpet creeper in the East and scarlet gilia in the West, have red flowers.

All sixteen species of hummingbirds that breed in North America nest in essentially the same way. Mating takes place after an elaborate courtship display by the male, in which the iridescent feathers on his throat or forehead glow like fire. After mating, the male and female separate, so the male will not compete for nectar with his own offspring. The female builds a small, snug, cuplike nest of plant down and cobweb, often decorated with bits of lichen to deflect raindrops, in which she lays from one to three white eggs. After an incubation period of about two weeks—nearly three weeks in the larger species—the eggs hatch and the female begins the frantic search for food. Young hummingbirds take up to four weeks to leave the nest and become independent. In most species, there is a second brood, and sometimes even a third, in a season.

Hummingbird species can be bewilderingly similar: most are tiny, mainly glossy green, the males with a bright "gorget" of red on the throat. But the species can be sorted out fairly easily by geography. Only the ruby-throated occurs in the eastern half of the United States. In the Northwest, a hummingbird that is mainly rusty is likely to be a rufous hummingbird. Along the California coast, Anna's hummingbird has a paler red throat and also has a red forehead, while Allen's hummingbird is smaller, with no red on the forehead and a rusty tinge to the breast and tail. In the Rocky Mountains, a hummingbird with a red throat is likely to be a broad-tailed, especially if its wings produce a distinct trill, but at high elevations it might be a Calliope hummingbird, a tiny creature whose throat is flecked with red rather than solid. In the mountains of southeastern Arizona, the broad-billed hummingbird—blue and green with a red bill—is a regular visitor to hummingbird feeders in the pine-oak woods. And in gardens in the Arizona desert, Costa's hummingbird has a throat patch that is purple, not red.

Wherever you live, you'll find at least one hummingbird species to enjoy, and you can attract them simply by putting out hummingbird feeders—available at any gardening store—or by planting their favorite flowers, such as fuchsia and monarda.

July 1994

		JULY				
S	M	T	W	T	F	S
					1	2
3	4	5	6	7	8	9
10	11	12	13	14	15	16
17	18	19	20	21	22	23
24/31	25	26	27	28	29	30

4 MONDAY   Independence Day

5 TUESDAY

6 WEDNESDAY

7 THURSDAY

8 FRIDAY   New Moon
                                   ●

9 SATURDAY

10 SUNDAY

Migratory pintails (*Anas acuta*), mallards (*Anas platyrhynchos*), and widgeons (*Anas americana*) taking flight at sunrise. Gray Lodge, Sacramento Valley Wetlands, California. Nikon FE2 with 400mm lens, Kodachrome 100 at F3.5. By Ron Sanford.

July 1994

		J U L Y			
S	M	T	W	T	F	S
					1	2
3	4	5	6	7	8	9
10	11	12	13	14	15	16
17	18	19	20	21	22	23
24/31	25	26	27	28	29	30

11 MONDAY

12 TUESDAY

13 WEDNESDAY

14 THURSDAY

15 FRIDAY

First Quarter

16 SATURDAY

17 SUNDAY

MONDAY *18*

TUESDAY *19*

WEDNESDAY *20*

THURSDAY *21*

Full Moon
○

FRIDAY *22*

SATURDAY *23*

SUNDAY *24*

July 1994

		JULY			
S	M	T	W	T	F	S
					1	2
3	4	5	6	7	8	9
10	11	12	13	14	15	16
17	18	19	20	21	22	23
24/31	25	26	27	28	29	30

25 MONDAY

26 TUESDAY

27 WEDNESDAY

28 THURSDAY

29 FRIDAY

30 SATURDAY   Last Quarter

31 SUNDAY

Tufted puffins (*Lunda cirrhata*). St. Paul Island, Alaska. Canon EOS 1 with 300mm lens, Fujichrome 100 at 1/125 second/F5.6. By Alissa Crandall.

Birding at the Shore

AUGUST IS a quiet time for land birds. Only a few species are still singing; most have raised their young, and birds are staying out of sight while they molt—exchanging their conspicuous breeding colors for the duller hues they will wear during the coming fall and winter. Some birds have already left for their wintering grounds. When things quiet down in the woods and fields, experienced birders head for the coast.

Here, too, the year's young have been raised, many birds are molting, and early migrants are beginning to trickle through. But habitats are more exposed along the coast, making birds easier to spot. For many birds of the shore, daily movements and patterns of activity are governed more by the rhythm of the tides than by that of sunrise and sunset. So birds can be seen throughout the day, not just at dawn, when land species are most active.

Shore habitats are more clearly defined than inland ones, making particular species easier to locate. Each species has a favorite feeding place. Many birds are found right at the water's edge, feeding on mud flats or sand. Sanderlings like to forage on the open beach, chasing each wave to catch tiny creatures before they duck back out of sight in the sand. Semipalmated plovers like to stalk across mud flats, using their large eyes to spot their prey and then darting forward to snatch it up. Yellowlegs, tall sandpipers with long legs, wade into the shallows for their food, but wading in deeper water is reserved for such large birds as the great blue heron.

Shoreline marshes, with their tall reeds and sedges, provide concealment for more bashful species. Bitterns, both the tall brown American bittern and the little buff-and-black least bittern, steal quietly through the vegetation in search of fish and crustaceans. Rails, slender marsh birds that have given us the expression "thin as a rail," slip between the reeds and marsh grasses in search of food. Even a few sparrows—seaside and sharp-tailed sparrows in the East and Savannah sparrows in the West—are specialized for life in marshes near the shore.

The cliffs of the Maritime Provinces, northern New England, and the Pacific coast offer some species safe, inaccessible nesting places and sites for easy take-off. Cormorants, gannets, brown pelicans, and kittiwakes all nest on ledges and forage on or over the water. Members of the auk family, including the gaudy tufted puffin, also like cliff-bound coasts, but some, among them the puffins, nest in burrows in the ground or the tops of the cliffs.

Many birds can be seen on the open water. Cormorants and auks are expert divers that pursue their prey beneath the waves. Other birds, including gulls, are adept at snatching food from the surface. Terns and gannets fly through the air watching the water for fish; the moment they spot their prey, they dive into the waves to seize it in their beaks. Ospreys also catch their prey by diving, but use their sharp talons instead of their bills to grasp slippery fish. Frigatebirds are pirates, chasing terns carrying fish until their victims drop their cargo and then swooping down to catch it before it hits the water.

Of all the birds that forage in flight over the waves, the black skimmer has the strangest feeding technique. The lower part of a skimmer's bill is longer than the upper, and as it flies along close to the surface, a skimmer uses this lower mandible to cut through the water like the blade of a knife. The instant the lower mandible touches a fish, the upper mandible snaps closed, and the prey is trapped.

August is not the only month for birding at the shore: there are many birds that appear there only during the winter. But on a hot summer day it is the best place to find birds, and so it is the best place to find birders.

August 1994

AUGUST						
S	M	T	W	T	F	S
	1	2	3	4	5	6
7	8	9	10	11	12	13
14	15	16	17	18	19	20
21	22	23	24	25	26	27
28	29	30	31			

1 MONDAY

2 TUESDAY

3 WEDNESDAY

4 THURSDAY

5 FRIDAY

6 SATURDAY

7 SUNDAY

New Moon

Great blue heron (*Ardea herodias*) at sunset. Gulf Island National Seashore, Florida. Mamiya 645 with 105–210mm zoom lens, Fujichrome 100 at 1/125 second/F5.6. By Jeff Foott.

August 1994

A U G U S T						
S	M	T	W	T	F	S
	1	2	3	4	5	6
7	8	9	10	11	12	13
14	15	16	17	18	19	20
21	22	23	24	25	26	27
28	29	30	31			

8 MONDAY

9 TUESDAY

10 WEDNESDAY

11 THURSDAY

12 FRIDAY

13 SATURDAY

14 SUNDAY

First Quarter

MONDAY *15*

TUESDAY *16*

WEDNESDAY *17*

THURSDAY *18*

FRIDAY *19*

SATURDAY *20*

Full Moon
○

SUNDAY *21*

August 1994

AUGUST						
S	M	T	W	T	F	S
	1	2	3	4	5	6
7	8	9	10	11	12	13
14	15	16	17	18	19	20
21	22	23	24	25	26	27
28	29	30	31			

22 MONDAY

23 TUESDAY

24 WEDNESDAY

25 THURSDAY

26 FRIDAY

27 SATURDAY

28 SUNDAY

Golden eagle (*Aquila chrysaetos*). Sierra Mountains near Woodleaf, California. Canon F-1 with 500mm lens, Kodachrome 64 at 1/250 second/F5.6. By John Hendrickson.

- The European starling is one of the most successful birds ever introduced into North America. The first ones were released in Central Park in 1890, and by 1950 the species had spread all the way to the Pacific Ocean.

- Red-eyed vireos have red eyes, but only when they are adults; young birds have brown eyes. The red-eyed vireo is such a persistent singer that it continues to sing even while it captures, subdues, and swallows large insects.

- A hovering hummingbird beats its wings 55 times a second, but in straight flight it may beat its wings 75 times a second.

- The mockingbird, once considered the quintessential bird of the Deep South, has recently been extending its range northward and now nests in Nova Scotia. These birds can copy the calls and songs of dozens of other species of birds, as well as human whistling, squeaky hinges, and barking dogs. But ornithologists still don't know why the birds do this, and are not fully convinced that mimicry is really involved.

- The so-called mute swan rarely calls but is not mute; in addition to hissing notes, it also has a puppylike bark.

- Most birds bathe by walking or hopping into the water, but birds that are mainly aerial, like swifts and terns, bathe by dipping into the water while in flight.

- Woodpeckers and brown creepers climb tree trunks by grasping the bark with their claws and using their tails as props. This means they must usually move upward. Nuthatches and the black-and-white warbler are more versatile. They don't use their tails as props but have very strong claws, so they can creep about on the bark in any direction, even moving head downward.

AUGUST						
S	M	T	W	T	F	S
	1	2	3	4	5	6
7	8	9	10	11	12	13
14	15	16	17	18	19	20
21	22	23	24	25	26	27
28	29	30	31			

SEPTEMBER						
S	M	T	W	T	F	S
				1	2	3
4	5	6	7	8	9	10
11	12	13	14	15	16	17
18	19	20	21	22	23	24
25	26	27	28	29	30	

August / September 1994

Last Quarter

◑

MONDAY 29

TUESDAY 30

WEDNESDAY 31

THURSDAY 1

FRIDAY 2

SATURDAY 3

SUNDAY 4

Hawk Flights

J U S T   A S the spring brings a dramatic warbler migration, fall yields a spectacular profusion of migrating birds of prey. An autumn day with a cool northwest wind, particularly if it follows a spell of warm, southerly winds, will send hundreds or even thousands of hawks, falcons, eagles, and ospreys on their way to the wintering grounds.

Birds of prey—or raptors—follow two kinds of flight paths during their southbound migration. Many travel along mountain ridges, while others move along the coast, skimming and soaring over cliffs, dunes, and salt marshes. In the East, where mountain ridges tend to run from northeast to southwest, a northwest wind will be deflected upward, so the migrating hawks can soar along effortlessly, buoyed up by the constant flow of air in this updraft. Often hundreds of broad-winged hawks, their wings outstretched and motionless, will form a slowly circling flock called a kettle, and drift southward riding an updraft, covering many miles with very little expenditure of energy.

Where mountain ridges come together, the migrants are funneled over a single spot, and thousands may pass in a single day. Such places used to be favorite resorts of gunners, who thought they were doing a good thing by killing these "chicken hawks" as they passed by. The most famous of these localities is Hawk Mountain on the Kittatinny Ridge in eastern Pennsylvania. There are reports of as many as five thousand hawks being killed in a single season at this one spot. Then, in 1934, Hawk Mountain was made a raptor sanctuary, the first of its kind, and the shooting stopped. Today tens of thousands of raptors pass Hawk Mountain unmolested every year.

Raptors following the coast use a different energy-saving technique. Where the sun strikes a smooth surface like hot sand in the dunes or a broad sandy beach, the warmed air rises, creating an upward current of air known as a thermal. Although coastal migrants do more actual flying than their mountain counterparts, they too conserve energy by riding one thermal after another as they make their way southward. They tend to avoid flying over water, which is cold and produces no thermals, but their route takes them across the entrances of Long Island Sound, Delaware Bay, and Chesapeake Bay. The best-known place for coastal hawk-watching on the East Coast is

Cape May, at the southern tip of New Jersey. Like Hawk Mountain in nearby Pennsylvania, it was once the scene of an annual hawk-shoot, but now it, too, is protected.

Birds of prey undertake their fall migration systematically, timing their departure to coincide with the disappearance or availability of their prey. Broad-winged hawks feed mainly on amphibians, and so they leave early, before a frost can send these aquatic animals underground or underwater for the winter. Sharp-shinned hawks prey on small birds, so their migration period is more extended, and they can feed easily along the way. Traveling sharp-shins can be seen during the entire hawk migration, both in the mountains and over the coastal dunes.

The birds that travel the farthest also leave first. Thus, the first migrants in September are likely to be broad-winged hawks, which winter in the tropics. With them are red-shouldered hawks, some sharp-shinned hawks, ospreys, and some bald eagles. The rest of the raptors follow in October and early November. October is the best month for seeing large numbers of peregrine falcons, kestrels, merlins, red-tailed hawks, more sharp-shinned hawks, Cooper's hawks, golden eagles, and northern goshawks; few of these later migrants leave the United States during the winter.

Because the hawk migration is so closely keyed to the weather, experienced hawk-watchers pay as much attention to the wind as anglers do to the tides. Even if you live near a famous hawk lookout, there is no point in visiting it if the winds are southerly. The time to go is when autumn weather is at its finest, with bright skies and a crisp breeze out of the north. A visit to a hawk lookout on a day like this is likely to give you a glimpse of one of the greatest wildlife spectacles North America has to offer.

September 1994

SEPTEMBER

S	M	T	W	T	F	S
				1	2	3
4	5	6	7	8	9	10
11	12	13	14	15	16	17
18	19	20	21	22	23	24
25	26	27	28	29	30	

5 MONDAY

New Moon

●

Labor Day

6 TUESDAY

Rosh Hashanah

7 WEDNESDAY

8 THURSDAY

9 FRIDAY

10 SATURDAY

11 SUNDAY

Female northern goshawk (*Accipiter gentilis*). Kent, Connecticut. Nikon FM2 with
50mm lens, Kodachrome 64 at 1/250 second/F8. By Jim Zipp.

September 1994

SEPTEMBER

S	M	T	W	T	F	S
				1	2	3
4	5	6	7	8	9	10
11	12	13	14	15	16	17
18	19	20	21	22	23	24
25	26	27	28	29	30	

12 MONDAY

First Quarter

13 TUESDAY

14 WEDNESDAY

15 THURSDAY

Yom Kippur

16 FRIDAY

17 SATURDAY

18 SUNDAY

Full Moon

○

MONDAY *19*

TUESDAY *20*

WEDNESDAY *21*

THURSDAY *22*

Equinox

FRIDAY *23*

SATURDAY *24*

SUNDAY *25*

September /
October 1994

		SEPTEMBER				
S	M	T	W	T	F	S
				1	2	3
4	5	6	7	8	9	10
11	12	13	14	15	16	17
18	19	20	21	22	23	24
25	26	27	28	29	30	

		OCTOBER				
S	M	T	W	T	F	S
						1
2	3	4	5	6	7	8
9	10	11	12	13	14	15
16	17	18	19	20	21	22
23/30	24/31	25	26	27	28	29

26 MONDAY

27 TUESDAY

Last Quarter

28 WEDNESDAY

29 THURSDAY

30 FRIDAY

1 SATURDAY

2 SUNDAY

Hermit thrush (*Catharus guttatus*) feeding on Russian olive tree berries
(*Elaeagnus angustifolia*). Robert Moses State Park, New York. Canon T90 with
500mm lens, Fujichrome 100 at 1/125 second/F9.5. By Harold Lindstrom.

Fall Migration

ONCE THE nesting season has come to a close, most birds spend a period of about a month feeding quietly and molting, replacing feathers that have been worn out during the strenuous activities associated with breeding. Then, as the days grow shorter and the nights grow cooler, they begin their fall migration. In the autumn, North America's bird population is at its peak; over half the birds heading southward are only a few months old, and when they head south, they are embarking on a journey they have never made before.

How do these birds know where to go? And how do they know how to get there? These questions have attracted the attention of ornithologists ever since the study of migration began, and now, after thousands of research papers have been written, we still don't fully understand the mystery of bird navigation. But we have learned a few things.

At least some birds navigate by using the stars. While they are still in the nest they watch the sky at night and identify the region around the Pole Star—where the stars remain in relatively fixed positions—as north. Later, during migration, their strategy is to fly away from the stationary Pole Star—that is, to fly south. The existence of this star compass was proved by an ornithologist who showed young indigo buntings a rotating sky map, one on which the wrong star—Betelgeuse in Orion—was made the stationary star. When the time for migration came, and these birds were shown the real sky, they tried to move away from Betelgeuse. Birds shown an accurate representation of the sky as nestlings navigated properly when it came time to migrate. Further proof of navigation by the stars may be provided by birds' reaction to the moon. It has been found that birds do not, as was formerly believed, use the moon in navigation. Experiments have shown that on nights when the moon is full birds navigate poorly, perhaps because the bright light of the moon makes it hard for them to detect the positions of stars.

But birds rely on other cues as well. On overcast nights they can still make their way southward by noting where the sun sets and orienting themselves so that they fly with the setting sun on their right, maintaining this flight direction after it is dark. On evenings when the sky is entirely overcast and the setting sun is not visible, birds either stay put or try to use the wind as a cue; but the wind is unreliable and likely to lead them in the wrong direction. In the daytime, birds, like bees, use the sun to navigate. Since the sun changes its position during the day, crossing the sky from east to west, solar navigation requires the existence of some as yet undiscovered internal time sense or biological clock. It has been found that some species, among them ring-billed gulls, indigo buntings, and Swainson's thrushes, can use the earth's magnetic field in navigation, and it may be that other migrants are sensitive to these weak magnetic cues. Birds may also use ultraviolet light, polarized light, barometric pressure, variations in gravity caused by the tides, and the patterns of waves on the sea to aid in navigation. Storm-petrels may even use odors to help them find their spring nesting islands.

Although birds are often seen following rivers and other landforms, there is no convincing evidence that birds use any topographic feature in navigation. They follow rivers only if other cues steer them to these routes. Still, the water thrush that reappears each fall in the same backyard in Venezuela, or the banded phoebe that shows up at the same bridge each spring, must recognize local landforms, even if these cues are not used over long distances.

We don't understand how birds know when they have migrated far enough, and we don't know how they find their way back to the same nesting place or even the same wintering spot, year after year. But these heroic annual journeys, charted by mysterious internal means, certainly show that birds live in a sensory world that is very different from our own.

October 1994

		OCTOBER				
S	M	T	W	T	F	S
						1
2	3	4	5	6	7	8
9	10	11	12	13	14	15
16	17	18	19	20	21	22
23/30	24/31	25	26	27	28	29

3 MONDAY

4 TUESDAY   New Moon
                                              ●

5 WEDNESDAY

6 THURSDAY

7 FRIDAY

8 SATURDAY

9 SUNDAY

Red-winged blackbirds (*Agelaius phoeniceus*) in flight. Bosque del Apache National Wildlife Refuge, New Mexico. Canon F-1 with 500mm lens, Fujichrome 100 at 1/1000 second/F5.6. By Darrell Gulin.

October 1994

OCTOBER

S	M	T	W	T	F	S
						1
2	3	4	5	6	7	8
9	10	11	12	13	14	15
16	17	18	19	20	21	22
23/30	24/31	25	26	27	28	29

10 MONDAY

Columbus Day *observed*
Thanksgiving (Canada)

11 TUESDAY

First Quarter
◑

12 WEDNESDAY

13 THURSDAY

14 FRIDAY

15 SATURDAY

16 SUNDAY

MONDAY *17*

TUESDAY *18*

WEDNESDAY *19*

Full Moon
◯

THURSDAY *20*

FRIDAY *21*

SATURDAY *22*

SUNDAY *23*

October 1994

OCTOBER

S	M	T	W	T	F	S
						1
2	3	4	5	6	7	8
9	10	11	12	13	14	15
16	17	18	19	20	21	22
23/30	24/31	25	26	27	28	29

24 MONDAY

25 TUESDAY

26 WEDNESDAY

27 THURSDAY   Last Quarter

28 FRIDAY

29 SATURDAY

30 SUNDAY   Daylight Saving Time Ends

Whooping crane (*Grus americana*) eating blue crab (*Callinectes sapidus*). Aransas
National Wildlife Refuge, Texas. Nikon F4 with 400mm lens, Kodachrome 64 at
1/250 second/F4.5. By Jeff Foott.

- Canada geese and certain other birds fly in wedge-shaped formations because the turbulence created by the flapping wings of each bird creates an uplift that enables the bird just behind it to save energy.

- In the fall, blackpoll warblers chart an odd triangular course, taking off from Cape Cod and flying southeastward straight over the Atlantic. When they reach the latitudes south of Bermuda, prevailing easterly winds shift their course and they land on the northern coast of South America. If it were not for these prevailing winds, they would be lost at sea when their energy stores gave out.

- The palm warbler, a familiar species early in spring migration, is rarely seen near palms. But its name is explained by the fact that the species was discovered on the island of Hispaniola in the West Indies, where palms are common.

- To conserve energy on cool nights, female hummingbirds sometimes place their nests beneath large leaves that block the escape of heat.

- During the winter, individual common loons defend a feeding territory in the daytime, but then gather into flocks on open water to spend the night.

- Tree swallows can survive the winter on a diet of energy-rich bayberries; this explains why, alone among the swallows, this species spends the winter as far north as Long Island.

- Every fall in southern Arizona gray-breasted jays bury thousands of acorns and then fail to retrieve them—thus helping to spread the oak woodlands on which the jays themselves depend.

- The red-headed woodpecker stores acorns and other nuts by wedging them into the rough bark of hickories and other trees, then returns during lean times in winter to hammer out the meat of the nuts.

October / November 1994

OCTOBER						
S	M	T	W	T	F	S
						1
2	3	4	5	6	7	8
9	10	11	12	13	14	15
16	17	18	19	20	21	22
23/30	24/31	25	26	27	28	29

NOVEMBER						
S	M	T	W	T	F	S
		1	2	3	4	5
6	7	8	9	10	11	12
13	14	15	16	17	18	19
20	21	22	23	24	25	26
27	28	29	30			

Halloween

MONDAY 31

TUESDAY 1

WEDNESDAY 2

New Moon
●

THURSDAY 3

FRIDAY 4

SATURDAY 5

SUNDAY 6

Birds in Danger

By November, the first of the whooping cranes have begun to arrive at their wintering grounds at Aransas National Wildlife Refuge on the coast of Texas. The whooping crane is the most celebrated of our endangered bird species, its population having dwindled to fifteen by 1937 because of habitat destruction and hunting. But today, thanks to careful monitoring of the population and a massive public education program, the number of birds that winter at Aransas and nest in Canada's Wood Buffalo National Park is well over one hundred and is augmented by a second flock, established during the 1980s, that nests in Idaho and spends the winter in New Mexico. The future now seems secure for the whooping crane.

But several other North American birds have suffered a harsher fate. Since the arrival of Europeans in North America, some have become extinct, including the great auk, Labrador duck, passenger pigeon, Carolina parakeet, and possibly the ivory-billed woodpecker. As humans continue to interfere with the natural world, additional species, unable to adapt to a rapidly changing environment, are declining in number, and some of these, designated as endangered or at least threatened, now receive special protection under the Endangered Species Act passed by Congress in 1973.

In the years after the Second World War, DDT and other hydrocarbons came to be widely used as crop pesticides. Since they all but eliminated crop-destroying insects, these chemicals were hailed as the solution to an age-old problem. But these same substances, once released into the environment, interfered with the calcium metabolism of many of the birds that stored the chemicals in their bodies. Egg shells became thinner, so such birds as the peregrine falcon, bald eagle, and osprey hawk began to suffer repeated nesting failure; when their populations started to plummet, DDT and its relatives were banned in North America, and now numbers of these striking birds of prey are building up again.

Even a seemingly harmless stroll on a beach can jeopardize some species. Piping plovers and least terns require clean, undisturbed beaches for nesting. Beach buggies and bathers have placed both of these species on the endangered list, and the only solution is the fencing off of every stretch of beach where these birds nest. Both of these little shore-dwelling birds are barely holding their own, and such elaborate protective measures may be necessary as long as people visit the nation's beaches during the summer.

The California condor has been declining for centuries, as the continent's big mammals, on whose carcasses it feeds, have gradually disappeared. Lead poisoning helped to eliminate the rest until, by late 1986, only three individuals could be found in the mountains north of Los Angeles. The remaining wild birds were trapped for their own safety and bred in captivity. With the captive breeding program a success, two condors were released in 1991, and there are now hopes of releasing more in the near future, and even of establishing a second population in the Grand Canyon.

The destruction of tropical rainforest, thousands of miles from the United States, has caused some species to be placed on the endangered list. The first victim of tropical deforestation was probably Bachman's warbler, a bird that once wintered in the lowland forest of Cuba and is now so rare that it is sighted only about once in a decade. As tropical forests continue to be cleared, more species will decline, and some scientists are again talking about a future "silent spring."

Habitat destruction in North America, too, is taking its toll. The draining and pollution of wetlands have decimated populations of wood storks and snail kites, and the clearing of old-growth southern pinelands has reduced the red-cockaded woodpecker to a remnant of its original numbers. Clearing of brushland in California has wiped out all but about 2,000 California gnatcatchers. Logging of old-growth forests in the Pacific Northwest has jeopardized the northern spotted owl and the marbled murrelet, the latter a seabird that flies inland to incubate its single egg on the branch of an ancient conifer. Even the fragmentation of woodlands in the northern states has meant increased predation on nesting birds—often the same ones that suffer from deforestation on their tropical wintering grounds.

As long as our technology continues to become more elaborate and our demands on the natural environment more intense, more bird species will be added to the endangered list. More and more species will come to require not only legal protection but constant supervision in order to survive.

November 1994

NOVEMBER

S	M	T	W	T	F	S
		1	2	3	4	5
6	7	8	9	10	11	12
13	14	15	16	17	18	19
20	21	22	23	24	25	26
27	28	29	30			

7 MONDAY

8 TUESDAY

Election Day

9 WEDNESDAY

10 THURSDAY

First Quarter

11 FRIDAY

Veterans Day
Remembrance Day (Canada)

12 SATURDAY

13 SUNDAY

Arctic peregrine falcon (*Falco peregrinus*). Hudson Bay, Manitoba, Canada. Nikon F4
with 80–200mm zoom lens, Fujichrome Velvia at 1/250 second/F5.6.
By Thomas D. Mangelsen.

November 1994

NOVEMBER

S	M	T	W	T	F	S
		1	2	3	4	5
6	7	8	9	10	11	12
13	14	15	16	17	18	19
20	21	22	23	24	25	26
27	28	29	30			

14 MONDAY

15 TUESDAY

16 WEDNESDAY

17 THURSDAY

18 FRIDAY

Full Moon

○

19 SATURDAY

20 SUNDAY

MONDAY *21*

TUESDAY *22*

WEDNESDAY *23*

Thanksgiving

THURSDAY *24*

FRIDAY *25*

Last Quarter
◑

SATURDAY *26*

SUNDAY *27*

November /
December 1994

NOVEMBER						
S	M	T	W	T	F	S
		1	2	3	4	5
6	7	8	9	10	11	12
13	14	15	16	17	18	19
20	21	22	23	24	25	26
27	28	29	30			

DECEMBER						
S	M	T	W	T	F	S
				1	2	3
4	5	6	7	8	9	10
11	12	13	14	15	16	17
18	19	20	21	22	23	24
25	26	27	28	29	30	31

28 MONDAY   Chanukah

29 TUESDAY

30 WEDNESDAY

1 THURSDAY

2 FRIDAY   New Moon

3 SATURDAY

4 SUNDAY

Green-winged teal drake (*Anas carolinensis*). Near Brainerd, Minnesota. Nikon F4 with 400mm lens, Fujichrome Velvia at 1/60 second/F8. By Bill Marchel.

Wild Ducks

DECEMBER IS the best month to spot North America's wild ducks and to begin learning to identify them. By then the waterfowl have completed their migrations and have arrived on their wintering grounds, where nearly all of them will be decked out in their most distinctive and colorful plumage. It is during this season that they sort themselves out most clearly according to habitat and feeding behavior.

The most distinctive and arguably the most beautiful of our ducks is the wood duck. The drake has dramatic markings of green, purple, chestnut, and buff, with face stripes of white and a crest. Wood ducks winter mainly in forested southern swamps, feeding on seeds, acorns, berries, and aquatic insects, but a few can be found each winter as far north as southern Canada.

The largest group of ducks is the dabblers, birds that feed on floating insects and vegetable matter at the surface or "tip up" with their tails pointing in the air as they reach for submerged plants. Dabblers include the mallard, the pintail, the gadwall, the shoveler, the wigeons, the green-winged teal, and other species of teal. These ducks like shallow water and are most commonly seen on ponds, in marshes, and on lakes with weedy margins.

Bay ducks are stockier than dabbling ducks, with heavier bodies well suited for diving. They gather in large flocks or "rafts" on bays and estuaries, where they dive for seeds, eelgrass, small clams, and snails. The bay ducks include the canvasback and redhead, both with glossy chestnut heads, the ring-necked duck, the lesser scaup, and its more northerly cousin, the greater scaup.

Birds with a life-style similar to that of the bay ducks are the two species of goldeneyes—so named for their bright yellow eyes—and their small black-and-white cousin, the bufflehead. These are chunky ducks that nest in holes in trees during the summer and spend the winter on bays and lakes, where they dive for crustaceans, mollusks, and some fish. The most widespread species is the common golden-eye, in which the drake has a dark, glossy green head and a large, round white spot in front of each eye. In flight, its wings make a loud whistling noise, giving rise to the hunter's name "whistler."

Sea ducks are a varied assortment of birds that may nest in the

Arctic but nearly always winter on salt water. The largest of these are the eiders, heavy-bodied birds that dive for marine animals; eiderdown, taken from their nests, is used as lining for jackets and parkas. The drakes are boldly clad in black and white, while the females are dark brown. The common and king eiders are found in winter on the rocky Atlantic and Pacific coastlines of the United States and Canada.

The three scoters—white-winged, surf, and black—are nearly as large as eiders and dive for mollusks and crustaceans as far south as the Gulf Coast in the East and California in the West. They often migrate single-file in large flocks, low over the waves, the line of birds extending as far as the eye can see in either direction.

Two other sea ducks are the harlequin duck, named for its clown-like pattern of spots and bars, and the oldsquaw, so named because of its garrulous calls during the spring mating season. Look for harlequin ducks along rocky coasts, where these little ducks are adept at prying mussels off the rocks, and watch for oldsquaws on any open body of salt water. Oldsquaws dive more deeply than any other duck; birds have been taken more than two hundred feet below the surface.

Mergansers are fish-eating divers with saw-toothed edges on their bills for grasping their slippery prey. There are three species, of which the red-breasted merganser is the only one that spends the winter almost exclusively on salt water. The common merganser, a large black-and-white duck with a glossy green head, prefers large ice-free rivers; the hooded merganser, whose drake has a white fan-shaped crest with a black border and is another candidate for most beautiful duck in North America, likes open ponds and lakes and quiet backwaters in rivers and salt marshes.

The ruddy duck is the most aquatic of our wild ducks. It prefers to avoid danger not by flying but by diving or by sinking quietly out of sight. It is common in winter only in the southern states, where it frequents marshes and weedy ponds to feed on insects or, especially in winter, on seeds and succulent water plants.

All these ducks can be seen by anyone willing to go out and look for them, but all have declined drastically during the last century because of the twin pressures of hunting and habitat destruction. Only the preservation of wetlands, such as the many sanctuaries maintained by the National Audubon Society, can save these beautiful birds from extinction.

December 1994

DECEMBER

S	M	T	W	T	F	S
				1	2	3
4	5	6	7	8	9	10
11	12	13	14	15	16	17
18	19	20	21	22	23	24
25	26	27	28	29	30	31

5 MONDAY

6 TUESDAY

7 WEDNESDAY

8 THURSDAY

9 FRIDAY   First Quarter

10 SATURDAY

11 SUNDAY

Lesser scaup (*Aythya affinis*). Upper Souris National Wildlife Refuge, North Dakota. Nikon F3 with 400mm lens, Kodachrome 64 at 1/500 second/F3.5. By Bill Vinje.

December 1994

DECEMBER

S	M	T	W	T	F	S
				1	2	3
4	5	6	7	8	9	10
11	12	13	14	15	16	17
18	19	20	21	22	23	24
25	26	27	28	29	30	31

12 MONDAY

13 TUESDAY

14 WEDNESDAY

15 THURSDAY

16 FRIDAY

17 SATURDAY — Full Moon ○

18 SUNDAY

MONDAY *19*

TUESDAY *20*

Solstice   WEDNESDAY *21*

THURSDAY *22*

FRIDAY *23*

SATURDAY *24*

Last Quarter   SUNDAY *25*

◑

Christmas

December 1994 /
January 1995

DECEMBER						
S	M	T	W	T	F	S
				1	2	3
4	5	6	7	8	9	10
11	12	13	14	15	16	17
18	19	20	21	22	23	24
25	26	27	28	29	30	31

JANUARY						
S	M	T	W	T	F	S
1	2	3	4	5	6	7
8	9	10	11	12	13	14
15	16	17	18	19	20	21
22	23	24	25	26	27	28
29	30	31				

26 MONDAY   Boxing Day (Canada)

27 TUESDAY

28 WEDNESDAY

29 THURSDAY

30 FRIDAY

31 SATURDAY

1 SUNDAY   New Moon

New Year's Day

Rufous-sided towhee (*Pipilo erythrophthalmus*). Issaquah, Washington. Canon F-1 with 500mm lens, Fujichrome 50 at 1/125 second/F8. By Darrell Gulin.

January 1995

JANUARY						
S	M	T	W	T	F	S
1	2	3	4	5	6	7
8	9	10	11	12	13	14
15	16	17	18	19	20	21
22	23	24	25	26	27	28
29	30	31				

2   MONDAY

3   TUESDAY

4   WEDNESDAY

5   THURSDAY

6   FRIDAY

7   SATURDAY

8   SUNDAY

First Quarter

Male swamp sparrow (*Melospiza georgiana*) singing. Dryden Lake, New York.
Nikon FE2 with 400mm lens, Fujichrome 50 at 1/125 second/F5.6. By Marie Read.

1993

JANUARY
S	M	T	W	T	F	S
					1	2
3	4	5	6	7	8	9
10	11	12	13	14	15	16
17	18	19	20	21	22	23
24	25	26	27	28	29	30
31						

FEBRUARY
S	M	T	W	T	F	S
	1	2	3	4	5	6
7	8	9	10	11	12	13
14	15	16	17	18	19	20
21	22	23	24	25	26	27
28						

MARCH
S	M	T	W	T	F	S
	1	2	3	4	5	6
7	8	9	10	11	12	13
14	15	16	17	18	19	20
21	22	23	24	25	26	27
28	29	30	31			

APRIL
S	M	T	W	T	F	S
				1	2	3
4	5	6	7	8	9	10
11	12	13	14	15	16	17
18	19	20	21	22	23	24
25	26	27	28	29	30	

MAY
S	M	T	W	T	F	S
						1
2	3	4	5	6	7	8
9	10	11	12	13	14	15
16	17	18	19	20	21	22
23	24	25	26	27	28	29
30	31					

JUNE
S	M	T	W	T	F	S
		1	2	3	4	5
6	7	8	9	10	11	12
13	14	15	16	17	18	19
20	21	22	23	24	25	26
27	28	29	30			

JULY
S	M	T	W	T	F	S
				1	2	3
4	5	6	7	8	9	10
11	12	13	14	15	16	17
18	19	20	21	22	23	24
25	26	27	28	29	30	31

AUGUST
S	M	T	W	T	F	S
1	2	3	4	5	6	7
8	9	10	11	12	13	14
15	16	17	18	19	20	21
22	23	24	25	26	27	28
29	30	31				

SEPTEMBER
S	M	T	W	T	F	S
			1	2	3	4
5	6	7	8	9	10	11
12	13	14	15	16	17	18
19	20	21	22	23	24	25
26	27	28	29	30		

OCTOBER
S	M	T	W	T	F	S
					1	2
3	4	5	6	7	8	9
10	11	12	13	14	15	16
17	18	19	20	21	22	23
24	25	26	27	28	29	30
31						

NOVEMBER
S	M	T	W	T	F	S
	1	2	3	4	5	6
7	8	9	10	11	12	13
14	15	16	17	18	19	20
21	22	23	24	25	26	27
28	29	30				

DECEMBER
S	M	T	W	T	F	S
			1	2	3	4
5	6	7	8	9	10	11
12	13	14	15	16	17	18
19	20	21	22	23	24	25
26	27	28	29	30	31	

1995

JANUARY
S	M	T	W	T	F	S
1	2	3	4	5	6	7
8	9	10	11	12	13	14
15	16	17	18	19	20	21
22	23	24	25	26	27	28
29	30	31				

FEBRUARY
S	M	T	W	T	F	S
			1	2	3	4
5	6	7	8	9	10	11
12	13	14	15	16	17	18
19	20	21	22	23	24	25
26	27	28				

MARCH
S	M	T	W	T	F	S
			1	2	3	4
5	6	7	8	9	10	11
12	13	14	15	16	17	18
19	20	21	22	23	24	25
26	27	28	29	30	31	

APRIL
S	M	T	W	T	F	S
						1
2	3	4	5	6	7	8
9	10	11	12	13	14	15
16	17	18	19	20	21	22
23	24	25	26	27	28	29
30						

MAY
S	M	T	W	T	F	S
	1	2	3	4	5	6
7	8	9	10	11	12	13
14	15	16	17	18	19	20
21	22	23	24	25	26	27
28	29	30	31			

JUNE
S	M	T	W	T	F	S
				1	2	3
4	5	6	7	8	9	10
11	12	13	14	15	16	17
18	19	20	21	22	23	24
25	26	27	28	29	30	

JULY
S	M	T	W	T	F	S
						1
2	3	4	5	6	7	8
9	10	11	12	13	14	15
16	17	18	19	20	21	22
23	24	25	26	27	28	29
30	31					

AUGUST
S	M	T	W	T	F	S
		1	2	3	4	5
6	7	8	9	10	11	12
13	14	15	16	17	18	19
20	21	22	23	24	25	26
27	28	29	30	31		

SEPTEMBER
S	M	T	W	T	F	S
					1	2
3	4	5	6	7	8	9
10	11	12	13	14	15	16
17	18	19	20	21	22	23
24	25	26	27	28	29	30

OCTOBER
S	M	T	W	T	F	S
1	2	3	4	5	6	7
8	9	10	11	12	13	14
15	16	17	18	19	20	21
22	23	24	25	26	27	28
29	30	31				

NOVEMBER
S	M	T	W	T	F	S
			1	2	3	4
5	6	7	8	9	10	11
12	13	14	15	16	17	18
19	20	21	22	23	24	25
26	27	28	29	30		

DECEMBER
S	M	T	W	T	F	S
					1	2
3	4	5	6	7	8	9
10	11	12	13	14	15	16
17	18	19	20	21	22	23
24	25	26	27	28	29	30
31						

1994

JANUARY

S	M	T	W	T	F	S
						1
2	3	4	5	6	7	8
9	10	11	12	13	14	15
16	17	18	19	20	21	22
23	24	25	26	27	28	29
30	31					

FEBRUARY

S	M	T	W	T	F	S
		1	2	3	4	5
6	7	8	9	10	11	12
13	14	15	16	17	18	19
20	21	22	23	24	25	26
27	28					

MARCH

S	M	T	W	T	F	S
		1	2	3	4	5
6	7	8	9	10	11	12
13	14	15	16	17	18	19
20	21	22	23	24	25	26
27	28	29	30	31		

APRIL

S	M	T	W	T	F	S
					1	2
3	4	5	6	7	8	9
10	11	12	13	14	15	16
17	18	19	20	21	22	23
24	25	26	27	28	29	30

MAY

S	M	T	W	T	F	S
1	2	3	4	5	6	7
8	9	10	11	12	13	14
15	16	17	18	19	20	21
22	23	24	25	26	27	28
29	30	31				

JUNE

S	M	T	W	T	F	S
			1	2	3	4
5	6	7	8	9	10	11
12	13	14	15	16	17	18
19	20	21	22	23	24	25
26	27	28	29	30		

JULY

S	M	T	W	T	F	S
					1	2
3	4	5	6	7	8	9
10	11	12	13	14	15	16
17	18	19	20	21	22	23
24	25	26	27	28	29	30
31						

AUGUST

S	M	T	W	T	F	S
	1	2	3	4	5	6
7	8	9	10	11	12	13
14	15	16	17	18	19	20
21	22	23	24	25	26	27
28	29	30	31			

SEPTEMBER

S	M	T	W	T	F	S
				1	2	3
4	5	6	7	8	9	10
11	12	13	14	15	16	17
18	19	20	21	22	23	24
25	26	27	28	29	30	

OCTOBER

S	M	T	W	T	F	S
						1
2	3	4	5	6	7	8
9	10	11	12	13	14	15
16	17	18	19	20	21	22
23	24	25	26	27	28	29
30	31					

NOVEMBER

S	M	T	W	T	F	S
		1	2	3	4	5
6	7	8	9	10	11	12
13	14	15	16	17	18	19
20	21	22	23	24	25	26
27	28	29	30			

DECEMBER

S	M	T	W	T	F	S
				1	2	3
4	5	6	7	8	9	10
11	12	13	14	15	16	17
18	19	20	21	22	23	24
25	26	27	28	29	30	31

Birding Resources

The following lists offer a sample of available birding resources.

FIELD GUIDES

The Audubon Society Field Guide to North American Birds: Eastern Region, by John Bull and John Farrand, Jr. New York: Alfred A. Knopf, 1977.

The Audubon Society Field Guide to North American Birds: Western Region, by Miklos D. F. Udvardy. New York: Alfred A. Knopf, 1977.

Audubon Society Master Guide to Birding, edited by John Farrand, Jr. 3 vols. New York: Alfred A. Knopf, 1983.

The Audubon Society Pocket Guides: Familiar Birds of North America, Eastern Region; Familiar Birds of North America, Western Region. Edited by Ann H. Whitman; Kenn Kaufman and John Farrand, Jr., consultants. New York: Alfred A. Knopf, 1986.

Birds of North America, revised edition, by Chandler S. Robbins, Bertel Bruun, and Herbert S. Zim. New York: Golden Press, 1983.

Field Guide to the Birds of North America, revised edition, by the National Geographic Society. Washington: National Geographic Society, 1987.

Roger Tory Peterson's Field Guide to Birds, 4th edition. Boston: Houghton Mifflin Co., 1980.

A Field Guide to Western Birds, by Roger Tory Peterson. Boston: Houghton Mifflin Co., 1990.

MAGAZINES

American Birds, 700 Broadway, New York, NY 10003

Audubon magazine, 700 Broadway, New York, NY 10003

Birding, American Birding Association, P. O. Box 31, Honeoye Falls, NY 14472

Bird Watchers Digest, P.O. Box 110, Marietta, OH 45750

Birder's World, 720 E. 8th St., Holland, MI 49423

Living Bird, Laboratory of Ornithology at Cornell University, 159 Sapsucker Woods Rd., Ithaca, NY 14850

Wild Bird, Fancy Publications, P.O. Box 6050, Mission Viejo, CA 92690

Wingtips, Box 226, Lansing, NY 14882

VIDEOGUIDES

The Audubon Society Videoguides to Birds of North America, vols. 1–5, Godfrey-Stadin Productions. Distributed by MasterVision, New York, NY 10028

The National Audubon Society's UP CLOSE Videos: Bluebirds; Cardinals; Hawks; Hummingbirds; Owls, Nature Science Network, Carrboro, NC 27510

For a list of all Audubon bird-related publications and products write:

> Licensing Department
> National Audubon Society
> 700 Broadway
> New York, NY 10003

The National Audubon Society

AT THE National Audubon Society,* our mission is to protect the wildlife and wildlife habitat upon which our lives depend. Together with more than 600,000 members and an extensive chapter network, our professional staff of scientists, lobbyists, lawyers, policy analysts, and educators is fighting to save threatened ecosystems and to restore the natural balance that is critical to the quality of life on our planet. Our underlying belief is that all forms of life are interdependent and that the diversity of nature is essential to both our economic and environmental well-being.

SANCTUARIES

Audubon, through its nationwide system of sanctuaries, protects more than a quarter-million acres of essential habitat and unique natural areas for birds, other wild animals, and rare plant life. The sanctuaries range in size from twelve acres around Theodore Roosevelt's grave in New York State to twenty-six thousand acres of coastal marsh in Louisiana. Most of the sanctuaries are staffed by resident wardens who also patrol adjacent natural areas not owned by Audubon.

CHAPTERS

Audubon's 600,000 members provide the underpinning for all the society's programs and activities. Two-thirds of our members also belong to local Audubon chapters, now numbering more than 500, which serve in their communities as focal points for conservation, nature education, and citizen action on environmental issues.

REGIONAL OFFICES

We also maintain regional and state offices staffed by full-time professional conservationists, who advance Audubon programs throughout the fifty states. Regional staff members guide and coordinate the varied activities of the many Audubon chapters, from operating na-

*National Audubon Society and Audubon are trademarks of the National Audubon Society, Inc.

ture centers to engaging in environmental litigation. They work on specific environmental issues and conduct leadership training workshops for citizen activists, to ensure the recruitment of a growing corps of citizen volunteers who are ready and able to participate effectively in the environmental policy process at every level of government.

GOVERNMENT RELATIONS

Through the staff of our Washington, D.C., office on Capitol Hill, Audubon maintains liaisons with federal agencies, testifies before Congress on legislative proposals related to our primary concerns, and pursues environmental litigation through court action to remedy threats to wildlife habitats. We also cooperate with other conservation organizations on local and national levels.

SCIENTIFIC ACTIVITIES

Our staff conducts wildlife research to aid endangered species such as the wood stork, the mountain lion, and the piping plover and to provide knowledge for the ecologically sound management of our sanctuaries. The work of these staff people is augmented by that of other scientists to ensure that our positions on such crucial environmental concerns as energy, global climate change, land use, water policy, and population have a sound, rational basis. We also employ consultants to review available data and to outline options on complex technical issues. We convene frequent conferences, workshops, and seminars to discuss and disseminate timely information on important environmental issues.

PUBLICATIONS

Our award-winning *Audubon* magazine, published six times a year, carries outstanding articles and color photography on wildlife and nature, and presents in-depth reports on critical environmental issues, as well as conservation news and comment. *Audubon* is sent to all members and, by subscription, to thousands of libraries, schools, and government agencies. Special members and supporters will also receive our monthly *Audubon Activist* newsjournal that keeps them up to date on environmental issues. We also publish *American Birds,* an ornithological journal that reports on the distribution, migration, and abundance of North American birds.

EDUCATION

Our educational staff provides information on environmental concerns in response to thousands of inquiries each month from our members and from the public. Through the educational activities of our chapters, thousands of young people are made aware of the natural world around them. We also operate education centers throughout the country. There, teacher-naturalists hold outdoor classes for schoolchildren and other groups, as well as provide outreach and teacher training at local schools and parks. Our summer ecology camps—in Maine, Connecticut, and Wyoming—provide intensive study sessions for adults and carry optional university credit. *Audubon Adventures,* a bimonthly four-page children's nature newspaper, reaches hundreds of thousands of elementary school students. The Audubon Expedition Institute offers travel-study programs in the United States for high school and college students.

TRAVEL

Audubon's travel program, with over twenty-five years of experience, sponsors more than twenty-five exciting trips every year to exotic places like Alaska, Antarctica, Baja California, Galapagos, Great Britain, Indonesia, Japan, and Patagonia. All tour operators must abide by our *Travel Ethic for Environmentally Responsible Travel,* and each trip is led by an experienced Audubon senior staff member.

TELEVISION

National Audubon Society Television Specials can be seen on cable station WTBS and public television stations. Accompanying books and educational computer software sets give viewers an opportunity for further study of the subjects covered by the television series.

LICENSED PRODUCTS

Audubon also has many licensed products, which, when purchased, help fund the programs mentioned above. These items include our award-winning calendars, holiday greeting cards, oversized books, field guides, video guides, porcelain figurines, binoculars, birdseed, bird feeders, stained glass, philatelics, Visa affinity credit card, T-shirts, jigsaw puzzles, beach towels, and scarves.

For more information about Audubon, write or call us at:
National Audubon Society
700 Broadway
New York, New York 10003
(212) 979-3000

NATIONAL AUDUBON SOCIETY HEADQUARTERS AND REGIONAL AND STATE OFFICES

National Headquarters
700 Broadway
New York, New York 10003
(212) 979-3000

Capital Office/Government Relations
666 Pennsylvania Avenue, SE
Washington, DC 20003
(202) 547-9009

National Education Office
(Headquarters)
Route 4, Box 171
Sharon, Connecticut 06069
(203) 364-0520

Science & Sanctuaries Division
Headquarters
Field Research Department
115 Indian Mount Trail
Tavernier, Florida 33070
(305) 852-5092

Alaska/Hawaii Regional Office
308 G Street, Room 217
Anchorage, Alaska 99501
(907) 276-7034

Hawaii State Office
212 Merchant St., Suite 320
Honolulu, Hawaii 96813
(808) 522-5566

Great Lakes Regional Office
(Illinois, Indiana, Kentucky, Michigan,
  Minnesota, Ohio, Wisconsin)
692 North High Street
Suite 208
Columbus, Ohio 43215
(614) 224-3303

Mid-Atlantic Regional Office
(Delaware, District of Columbia,
  Maryland, New Jersey, Pennsylvania,
  Virginia, West Virginia)

1104 Fernwood Avenue, Suite 300
Camp Hill, Pennsylvania 17011
(717) 763-4985

Minnesota State Office and Audubon
  Council
26 East Exchange Street
Suite 207
St. Paul, Minnesota 55101
(612) 225-1830

New Mexico State Office
Randall Davey Audubon Center
P.O. Box 9314
Santa Fe, New Mexico 87504
(505) 983-4609

Northeast Regional Office
(Connecticut, Maine, Massachusetts,
  New Hampshire, New York, Rhode
  Island, Vermont)
1789 Western Avenue
Albany, New York 12203
(518) 869-9731

Rocky Mountain Regional Office
(Arizona, Colorado, Idaho, Montana,
  Utah, Wyoming)
4150 Darley Avenue, Suite 5
Boulder, Colorado 80303
(303) 499-0223/0219

Southeast Regional Office
(Alabama, Florida, Georgia, Mississippi,
  North Carolina, Puerto Rico, South
  Carolina, Tennessee)
102 East Fourth Avenue
Tallahassee, Florida 32303
(904) 222-2473

Southwest Regional Office
(Louisiana, Guatemala, Mexico, New
  Mexico, Panama, Texas)
2525 Wallingwood, Suite 1505
Austin, Texas 78746
(512) 327-1943/1946

Vermont/Maine State Office
Fiddler's Green, Box 9
Waitsfield, Vermont 05673
(802) 496-5727

Washington State Office
P.O. Box 462
Olympia, Washington 98507
(206) 786-8020

West Central Regional Office
(Arkansas, Iowa, Kansas, Missouri,
  Nebraska, North Dakota, Oklahoma,
  South Dakota)
200 South Wind Place, Suite 205
Manhattan, Kansas 66502
(913) 537-4385

Western Regional Office
(California, Guam, Nevada, Oregon,
  Washington)
555 Audubon Place
Sacramento, California 95825
(916) 481-5332

EDUCATION CENTERS AND OFFICES

National Center for Environmental
  Education
Audubon Center in Greenwich
613 Riversville Road
Greenwich, Connecticut 06831
(203) 869-5272

National Audubon Society
New York Education Office
700 Broadway
New York, New York 10003
(212) 979-3000

Audubon Center of the Northwoods
Route 1
Sandstone, Minnesota 55072
(612) 245-2648

Northeast Audubon Center
Route 4, Box 171
Sharon, Connecticut 06069
(203) 364-0520

Audubon Expedition Institute
P.O. Box 170
Readfield, Maine 04355
(207) 685-4333

Randall Davey Audubon Center
P.O. Box 9314
Sante Fe, New Mexico 87504
(505) 983-4609

Aullwood Audubon Center and Farm
1000 Aullwood Road
Dayton, Ohio 45414
(513) 890-7360

Richardson Bay Audubon Center
376 Greenwood Beach Road
Tiburon, California 94920
(415) 388-2524

National Audubon Society
Los Angeles Education Office
200 Culver Boulevard
Playa del Rey, California 90293
(310) 574-2799

Schlitz Audubon Center
1111 East Brown Deer Road
Milwaukee, Wisconsin 53217
(414) 352-2880

WILDLIFE SANCTUARIES

National Audubon Society Sanctuary
  Department Headquarters
93 West Cornwall Road
Sharon, Connecticut 06069
(203) 364-0048

Borestone Mountain Sanctuary
Box 112
Monson, Maine 04464
(207) 997-3607 (summer)
(207) 997-3558 (winter)

Francis Beidler Forest Sanctuary
Route 1, Box 600
Harleyville, South Carolina 29448
(803) 462-2150/2160

Clyde E. Buckley Sanctuary
Route 3, 1305 Germany Road
Frankfort, Kentucky 40601
(606) 873-5711

Constitution Marsh Sanctuary
RFD #2, Route 9D
Garrison, New York 10524
(914) 265-2601

Corkscrew Swamp Sanctuary
Route 6, Box 1875-A
Sanctuary Road
Naples, Florida 33964
(813) 657-3771/4662

Dauphin Island Sanctuary
P.O. Box 189
Dauphin Island, Alabama 36528
(205) 861-2882

Richardson Bay Audubon Center and
    Sanctuary
376 Greenwood Beach Road
Tiburon, California 94920
(415) 388-2524

Theodore Roosevelt Sanctuary
134 Cove Road
Oyster Bay, New York 11771
(516) 922-3200

Sabal Palm Grove
P.O. Box 5052
Brownsville, Texas 78523
(512) 541-8034

Science and Field Research Offices

Ecosystems Research Unit
Route 6, Box 1877
Naples, Florida 33964
(813) 657-2531

Scully Science Center
550 South Bay Avenue
Islip, New York 11751
(516) 224-3730

Puffin Project
Fratercula Fund and Seabird Restoration
    Program
159 Sapsucker Woods Road
Ithaca, New York 14850
(607) 257-7308 (summer)
(207) 529-5828 (winter)

Membership in the National Audubon Society will bring you...

- One year (six bimonthly issues) of award-winning *Audubon* magazine.
- Membership in your local Audubon chapter and participation in its exciting programs and special events.
- The opportunity to visit Audubon Nature Centers and Sanctuaries and to attend Audubon Ecology Camps and Workshops.
- Opportunity for complimentary membership in the Audubon Activist Network, including a subscription to the *Audubon Activist* newsjournal.
- Eligibility for wide-ranging Audubon tours.
- Books, gifts, and collectibles of particular interest to nature lovers.
- The satisfaction of knowing that your membership helps support sanctuaries, field research, environmental education, environmental legislation, and other efforts critical to the protection of wildlife and the environment.

MEMBERSHIP APPLICATION

Yes, I want to join the
NATIONAL AUDUBON SOCIETY

Enroll me as a member, start my subscription to *Audubon,* and send me my membership card, which entitles me to all the benefits and privileges of National Audubon Society membership.

Please make check payable to National Audubon Society and mail to Membership Data Center, P.O. Box 52529, Boulder, Colorado 80322-2529.

The special introductory rate is $20. I save $15!

☐ Check enclosed ☐ Please bill me

Name _____

Address _____

City _____ State _____ Zip _____

5ETM3